THE YOUNG ADULT'S GUIDE TO

IDENTITY THEFT

A Step-by-Step Guide to Stopping Scammers

BY MYRA FAYE TURNER

FOREWORD BY
AXTON BETZ-HAMILTON, PH.D., AFC®

THE YOUNG ADULT'S GUIDE TO IDENTITY THEFT: A STEP-BY-STEP GUIDE TO STOPPING SCAMMERS

Copyright © 2016 Atlantic Publishing Group, Inc.

1405 SW 6th Avenue • Ocala, Florida 34471 • Phone 800-814-1132 • Fax 352-622-1875
Website: www.atlantic-pub.com • Email: sales@atlantic-pub.com
SAN Number: 268-1250

Library of Congress Cataloging-in-Publication Data

Names: Turner, Myra Faye, author.
Title: The young adult's guide to identity theft : a step-by-step guide to stopping scammers / by Myra Faye Turner.
Description: Ocala : Atlantic Publishing Group, Inc., [2017] | Includes bibliographical references and index.
Identifiers: LCCN 2016050057 (print) | LCCN 2017001683 (ebook) | ISBN 9781620231791 (alk. paper) | ISBN 1620231794 (alk. paper) | ISBN 9781620231807 (ebook)
Subjects: LCSH: Identity theft. | Identity theft—Prevention.
Classification: LCC HV6675 .T87 2017 (print) | LCC HV6675 (ebook) | DDC 332.024—dc23
LC record available at https://lccn.loc.gov/2016050057

Printed in the United States

PROJECT MANAGER: Rebekah Sack • rsack@atlantic-pub.com
INTERIOR LAYOUT AND JACKET DESIGN: Nicole Sturk • nicolejonessturk@gmail.com

Reduce. Reuse.
RECYCLE.

A decade ago, Atlantic Publishing signed the Green Press Initiative. These guidelines promote environmentally friendly practices, such as using recycled stock and vegetable-based inks, avoiding waste, choosing energy-efficient resources, and promoting a no-pulping policy. We now use 100-percent recycled stock on all our books. The results: in one year, switching to post-consumer recycled stock saved 24 mature trees, 5,000 gallons of water, the equivalent of the total energy used for one home in a year, and the equivalent of the greenhouse gases from one car driven for a year.

Over the years, we have adopted a number of dogs from rescues and shelters. First there was Bear and after he passed, Ginger and Scout. Now, we have Kira, another rescue. They have brought immense joy and love not just into our lives, but into the lives of all who met them.

We want you to know a portion of the profits of this book will be donated in Bear, Ginger and Scout's memory to local animal shelters, parks, conservation organizations, and other individuals and nonprofit organizations in need of assistance.

– Douglas & Sherri Brown,
President & Vice-President of Atlantic Publishing

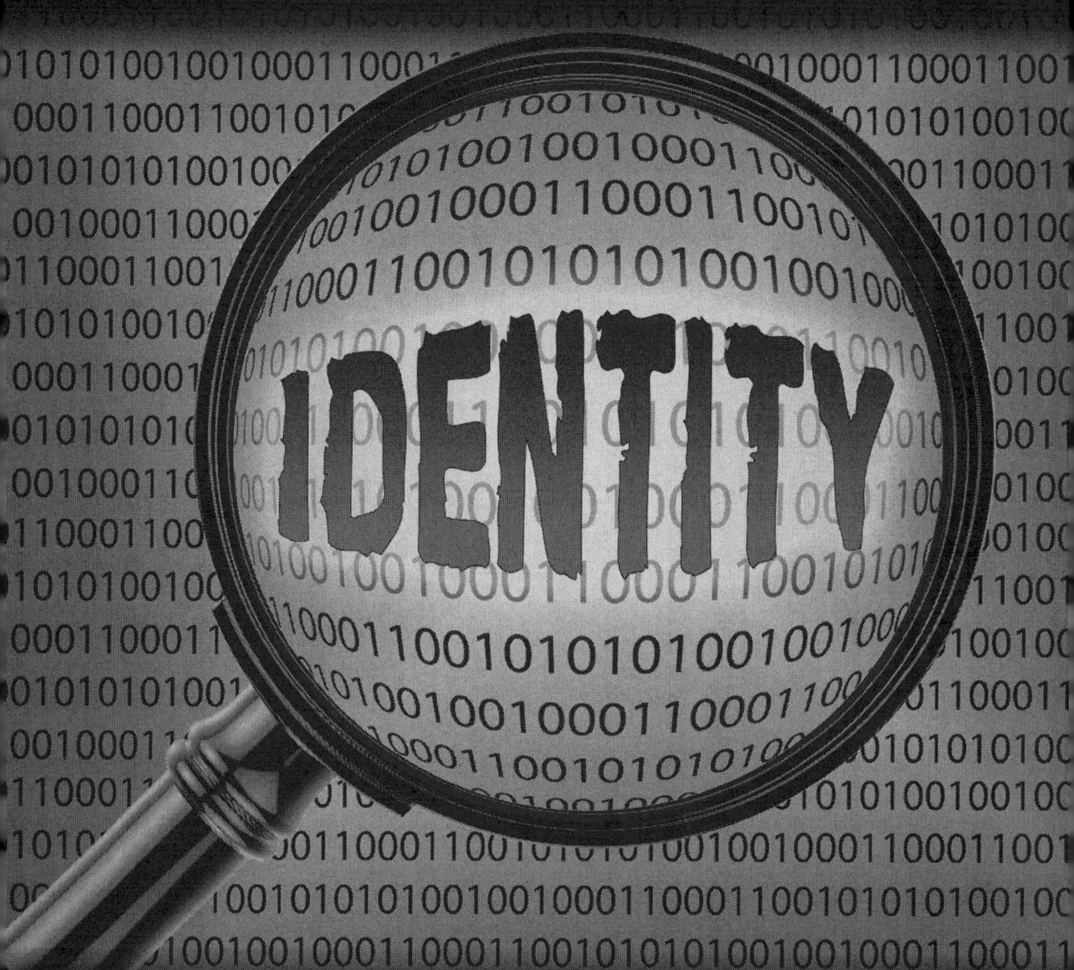
IDENTITY

Table of Contents

A s an Assistant Professor of Consumer Studies at Eastern Illinois University, I conduct research on child identity theft and financial exploitation within families. I also teach courses in the areas of personal finance and financial counseling. Both of these courses cover information on identity theft. Also, I am frequently interviewed by national media about child identity theft. As an expert on this topic, I can assure you the information you are about to read is thorough and accurate. An additional "bonus" for you is that you will be learning information that many of my students are not exposed to until they are in college—you're getting a head start!

In addition to my professional background, I was a victim of identity theft as a young adult. My identity was stolen at the age of 11, and I didn't know I was a victim until I tried to establish electric service at my first apartment when I was 19. Technically, I am considered an "adult/child" identity theft victim as my identity was stolen while I was under the age of 18, but I didn't learn I was a victim until after I had turned 18. My personal experience with identity theft helped launch my professional career, and my research on child identity theft helped me discover who had stolen my identity 20 years after it was stolen.

In my case, the thief was my mom, and she didn't just steal my identity— she had stolen my dad's identity and my grandpa's identity as well. Given this revelation, I am also a victim of familial identity theft, which is when a family member steals your identity. You will learn more about familial identity theft in Chapter 8, including how to deal with it, should it happen to you. If you know you are a victim of familial identity theft, this book offers excellent advice, including how to cope with possible changes in family dynamics as a result of filing charges against the thief.

If you are a victim of identity theft and are under age 18, share this book with your parent or guardian as they will be tasked with working to restore your identity. While you are under 18, there is not much you can do to address any damage that an identity thief causes—leave that for your parent or guardian. If you are 18 or older and are a victim of identity theft, keep this book handy and refer to it as you work to reclaim your identity.

If you are not a victim of identity theft, put the advice offered in this book to use, one step at a time. For example, if you don't have an anti-virus software installed on your computer, cell phone, or other electronic devices, install it to protect yourself from malware. Implementing the suggestions provided one step at a time will minimize your chances of becoming an identity theft victim, and you won't feel overwhelmed.

—Axton Betz-Hamilton, Ph.D., AFC®

Axton Betz-Hamilton, Ph.D., AFC®, is an Assistant Professor of Consumer Studies at Eastern Illinois University (EIU) in Charleston, Illinois. At EIU, she teaches courses on personal finance, financial counseling, and housing. She also conducts research on financial exploitation within families as well as child identity theft. Her personal experiences as a victim of identity theft along with her professional expertise have been featured on a variety of media outlets, including the Australian Broadcasting Corporation, Raidió Teilifís Éireann (Ireland), NBC News, The Huffington Post, and the Radiotopia podcast "Criminal."

Introduction

I t was the middle of a wet week. But not even the rain could dampen 16-year-old Riley's spirits. Today was the day she had been waiting for since — *forever*. Riley was about to start a new chapter in her life, a first step toward adulthood. She was about to land her first job.

Riley had done all of the prep work. She bought a book on job interviewing and read it cover to cover. She had a clean, crisp, nicely-formatted copy of her résumé. Her mom had helped her practice her interviewing skills by playing the part of a hiring manager. She felt relaxed and confident.

Riley put on a freshly pressed suit and headed out the door. She arrived for the interview 15 minutes early — emphasizing that punctuality is a trait she definitely possessed.

As expected, the interview went well. Riley's future boss, Mr. Smith, is impressed with her. He makes a job offer pending the outcome of a background check. No worries — she has never been in any legal trouble. She fills out the required paperwork and then returns home.

A day later, the tight seams of Riley's life start to unravel. She receives a call:

Mr. Smith: Hi Riley, I'm sorry to have to do this but—I really have no choice. I'm rescinding the job offer.

With head-scratching confusion, Riley asks Mr. Smith why he yanked the rug from under her feet:

Riley: I don't understand. I thought I had a good interview.

Mr. Smith: No, it wasn't the interview. You did an excellent job, and I believe you would be a great addition to our team. But, when we ran a background check, several red flags popped up.

Riley: Red flags? Like what?

Mr. Smith: Well, um, you or someone with your Social Security number has a large amount of debt—over $125,000—and all of the accounts are in collection.

Riley: That's not possible.

Mr. Smith: I'm afraid there's more. There's also an arrest warrant against you for failing to appear in court.

Riley: No way! This is all a huge mistake. Can you run my number again? Maybe the wrong number was entered?

Mr. Smith: "We checked twice with the same results. So, unless you gave us the wrong number, the debt and the warrant are attached to your name."

After verifying that Mr. Smith had the correct Social Security number, Riley felt like a deflated birthday balloon. Although Mr. Smith sympathized with Riley, he explained that company policy would not allow him to offer her a position.

After ending the short, unpleasant conversation, Riley tells her mom what happened. Her mom thinks she knows what the problem is, but she can't be sure. After a bit of investigating, her suspicions are verified. Riley is the victim of identity theft.

Someone stole Riley's Social Security number and used it to get a fake driver's license, buy an apartment, and rack up a huge amount of debt in her name. Social Security numbers are as individual as fingerprints, but now, Riley and the thief's identities are blended together like a gooey grilled cheese sandwich.

This thief also skipped out on a court appearance—an appearance on the court docket because of a driving while intoxicated (DWI) arrest. Not only is Riley's credit ruined, but there are legal issues that need ironing out.

Although this is bad news, Riley thinks there may be a silver lining. She calls Mr. Smith and explains what happened, hoping she can still get her dream job. Unfortunately, Mr. Smith says he still can't offer Riley a position. At least, not until she "sorts things out."

Six months later, Riley is still trying to sort things out. She was not able to pinpoint when her Social Security number was stolen or who stole it. All of the accounts were less than a year old, though. Her mom sent for a copy of Riley's credit report—a report neither knew existed—to get a better idea of the damage.

A credit report is a summary of your financial accounts. Lenders, such as banks and credit card companies, use credit reports to decide if they want to give you money. Your credit report shows which accounts you have and whether you pay them on time. In the past, it was customary for any position that involved handling cash to require a credit check. But today, many employers also will request your credit report before deciding whether to offer you a job. Bad debts can stick to you like a bandage on a scabby knee.

Riley's report verified what Mr. Smith told her. The thief had opened several accounts in her name, which were all in collections. Riley had to jump through a lot of hoops to clear her name, including proving she wasn't the "Riley" arrested for DWI.

Riley's life has been turned upside down because of identity theft.

WHAT IS IDENTITY THEFT?

Identity theft is one of the fastest growing crimes in the United States. If you become a victim, it may take months or even years to get your life back on the right track.

Before we take a look at how you can protect your identity, let's make sure everyone is on the same page. What does it mean when someone steals your identity? Let's start with a dictionary definition.

The Merriam-Webster dictionary defines identity theft as "The illegal use of someone else's personal identifying information (such as a Social Security number) in order to get money or credit."[1]

So, in most cases, when someone steals your identity, they aren't running around pretending that they are you. That's the good news. The bad news is they want the money you already have or plan to open new accounts in your name.

There are a few oddball exceptions. There was the case of the 33-year-old mother who pretended she was her 15-year-old daughter. I swear I'm not making this up. According to an article by Jeff Maysh on the Atlantic.com website, in 2008, Wendy Brown stole her daughter's identity.[2] Brown enrolled in high school—and check this out— she even tried out for the cheerleading squad! And, yes, she made the team.

In this book, however, we're going to focus on the crime of identity theft, where the goal is relieving you of the money or credit that you already have or sinking you in debt by opening new accounts. We will also touch on other ways your sensitive information may be used, like getting a fake driver's license. But first, let's take a look at how serious identity theft is.

STATISTICS ON IDENTITY THEFT

Now that you have a clear understanding of what identity theft is, maybe you're thinking it's not a big deal. "Identity theft is rare," you say. Unfortunately, that's not the case. Every year, millions of people have their identity stolen. In a recent report by Javelin Strategy & Research, 13.1 million

---

1. Merriam-Webster Online Dictionary, 2016
2. Maysh, 2016

people in the U.S. were victims of identity theft.[3] The cost? $15 billion. Those are some serious numbers.

A 2015 report by the Federal Trade Commission (FTC) says that identity theft was at the top of the list of consumer complaints for the 15th consecutive year. [4] The numbers are probably a lot higher. Some people aren't aware they have been victimized. Others refuse to report the thefts— especially if their foolishness resulted in their being scammed. Still others will not report the crime because they know the perpetrator. Either way, I think it is safe to say that identity theft is huge problem.

WHO IS AT RISK FOR IDENTITY THEFT?

Let's take a short quiz. Which of the following is more likely to have their identity stolen?

a) Your grandparents

b) Your 6-year-old cousin

c) Your neighbor's dead father

d) You

e) All of the above

If you choose **e**, you are one smart cookie. In a word—everyone is at risk (okay, that was actually four words). When I say everyone, I mean everyone. This includes adults, babies, teens, young adults—even dead people.

"Wait. Hold up. Did you say, dead people?"

---

3. Javelin Strategy & Research, 2016
4. Federal Trade Commission, 2015

Yes, I did. Dead men tell no tales and, apparently, do not check their credit report either. The easiest way for crooks to steal a dead person's identity is immediately after their death. Once they get their paws on the dearly departed's Social Security number, they will quickly rack up a bunch of debt before anyone catches on.

This happens more often than you would imagine. A typical scenario plays out like this:

1) A thief gets access to a dead person's Social Security number.

2) *Wham*—they either open new accounts and run up a bunch of debt quickly, or they squeeze as much juice as they can from existing accounts.

3) Since it sometimes takes a while to report that someone has died, the thief can cause a lot of damage in the meantime.

When the family finds out, they will have to move quickly to stop further damage. It's bad enough having to deal with the loss of a loved one— imagine having to iron out stolen identity issues, too.

Deceased residents of retirement communities and nursing homes are prime targets for identity theft. Often the people responsible for their care are also responsible for the theft. If the deceased does not have a family, the facility (or an employee) may simply not report the death. They will con- tinue to cash their Social Security checks, too. This is in addition to clean- ing out their bank accounts or opening new credit accounts.

HOW DO I USE THIS BOOK?

So you want to know more about protecting yourself from becoming a victim of identity theft? Great, you have already taken the first step—you are reading this book. Think of this book as your roadmap on your journey to educate yourself about identity theft. Armed with the right information, you can stop most scammers from stealing your identity.

So where do we go from here? You could jump ahead to Chapter 6 to learn how to protect yourself from becoming a victim. But that would be like taking a driving exam without ever setting foot in a car. There are still a few things you should know first.

So, the first thing we are going to do is learn about Internet safety and the history of identity theft (Chapter 1). In Chapter 2, we will look closer at the reasons why young people are often the target for identity theft. Plus, we will find out who's stealing identities—and, most importantly, why.

Chapter 3 takes a closer look at typical ways scammers try to steal your identity online. And just in case you thought offline criminals aren't hard at work looking for ways to steal your identity, Chapter 4 looks at old-school identity theft tactics.

Chapter 5 will highlight common scams often aimed at teens. When we arrive at Chapter 6, you will be glad you did not skip ahead. At this point, your head will be bursting with all of the good stuff you learned in the previous chapters. This important chapter will offer tips on how to stay safe online *and* in the real world.

Despite the best precautions, sometimes your identity is still stolen. But don't worry; Chapter 7 will instruct you on what to do if it happens to you. I mentioned earlier that there are times when the victim knows the perpetrator. In Chapter 8, we take a look at what you should do when the perp is a family member or friend. Unfortunately, this happens more often that you would expect. Finally, the last chapter discusses various types of identity theft protection safeguards.

Your complete guide to identity theft is waiting. So, turn the page and let's begin.

CHAPTER 1
How Safe Is the Internet?

How much time do you spend online? If you are like most young adults, the answer is probably "Too many hours to count." Whether you're posting to your social media accounts, checking out the latest Lil Uzi Vert video on YouTube, or streaming music on Spotify, you're probably connected most of your waking hours (and a few of your non-waking hours).

I know it may seem like the Internet is relatively new, but this technology has been around for a while. What evolved into the Internet we know and love today started out in the 1960s as ARPAnet—a system created by the government to allow their computers to communicate with each other.

I fondly remember the first time I logged on after signing up with American Online (AOL). I am less fond of the ear screeching dial-up cries from the modem. I remember not sleeping that first night (it's okay, I was on vacation). I was so entranced with the "World Wide Web" I did not want to sign off.

Thankfully, over time I became less addicted to the web. But, like most of us, I can't imagine a life without the Internet. It is definitely a great time we live in. We can connect with a friend who lives just around the corner. We can keep in touch with a loved one who lives across the country—or on the other side of the globe. And we "friend" people who we will probably never meet face-to-face. This connectivity is great, but sometimes there is a price to pay. It's called identity theft.

HOW SERIOUS IS IDENTITY THEFT?

Before we get to the nuts and bolts of how to stop scammers in their tracks, let's take a closer look at just how serious identity theft is. I have already given you some numbers, but maybe you're still thinking, "It can't happen to me." Think again.

As more people spend time online, we can expect the number of stolen identities to continue to rise. Scammers spend many hours thinking up sophisticated ways to steal your identity. A criminal may steal your identity as a crime of opportunity. A family member may feel they have no choice but to use your identity when they're in a jam.

I don't want to scare you; I simply want to make you aware. You do not have to give up your favorite Internet activities. What this book will show you is how to protect yourself while you are surfing the web. This book will arm you with the tools you need to protect yourself.

So back to my original question. How serious is identity theft? Let's look at some recently prosecuted fraud cases reported by the Internal Revenue Service (IRS):

- A North Carolina couple was sentenced to 324 months (the wife) and 70 months (the husband) in prison for using illegally-obtained information to file false tax returns. The couple also had to pay the Internal Revenue Service (IRS) $3,978,211 in restitution. Restitution typically means you pay back what you took, so we can assume the couple received over $3 million from their illegal scheme.

- A Georgia man filed over 5,000 false tax returns using information he scammed from victims by claiming they could receive money through two government programs. He was sentenced to 240 months in prison and had to pay $5,041,869 in restitution. He had another $4,185,455 in different bank accounts, which he had to forfeit.

- An Ohio man preyed on low-income and unemployed single parents in a scheme to obtain personal information. He then used this information to file 977 false tax returns. His sentence was 100 months in prison and $3,517,534 in restitution.

- This case is disturbing because it involves a bogus charity. An Ohio man created a sham charity and solicited donations by using advertising to direct donors to his website. Using the names and Social Security numbers provided by the donors, he filed over 500 false tax returns. He was sentenced to 108 months in prison and ordered to pay $1,457,936 in restitution.[5]

As you can see, identity theft is a serious crime. These examples only highlight crooks that file false tax returns, but many more use stolen identities to open new accounts, take out loans, commit crimes, and generally wreak havoc with someone else's life. Sometimes when your identity is stolen, you may receive partial reimbursements for your loss. The remaining loss is your "out of pocket" expense. Findings from a report released by the Bureau of Justice Statistics (BJS), shows that 14 percent of identity theft victims in 2014 had out of pocket losses of $1,000 or more.[6]

But how did we get here? Read on to find out.

THE EVOLUTION OF IDENTITY THEFT

People have been stealing identities since Jacob pretended he was his brother Esau in the book of Genesis. These spirited twins gave their mom Rebekah all kinds of trouble, twisting and fighting while still in the womb.

But it didn't stop there. You know when twins are born, one has to make an appearance first. The older twin (if only "older" by a few minutes) will often taunt the younger sibling like this:

> **Older twin:** You better listen to me, I'm your older brother.
> **Younger twin:** You're not the boss of me. You're only one minute older than I am.
> **Older twin:** I'm still your older brother!

---

5. Internal Revenue Service, 2015
6. Bureau of Justice Statistics, 2015

In this story, Esau was born first and Jacob came next—clinging to his brother's heel. I'm not sure what that was all about, but it was a pretty good indication that Jacob was going to be a troublemaker.

Now back in biblical days, you could pretty much count on either someone handing down a prophesy or God giving you the lowdown on what you could expect. That is exactly what happened in this case.

Word on the street was "the elder (Esau) would serve the younger (Jacob)." But the twins' father Isaac was having none of that. Parents aren't supposed to have a favorite child—but let's face it, they usually do. Because Isaac favored Esau, he wanted him to one day become ruler.

The struggle between the brothers was real. They were different as night and day. Esau was a rugged outdoorsy type who liked to hunt. His brother preferred hanging out in tents. There wasn't much twinning going on between these two.

While their father Isaac favored Esau, their mother Rebekah was partial to Jacob. Years passed, and eventually Isaac grew old and blind. He sensed his days were numbered and wanted to bless Esau before it was too late.

One day, he called Esau into his tent:

> **Isaac:** My beloved son, I feel my days are growing short. Before I go, can you do me a solid? Run out and kill a deer for me.
> **Esau:** *Ookay.*

Isaac told Esau that he wanted him to grill that sucker until it was all sizzling hot and melt-in-your-mouth scrumptious. Isaac promised that, once his belly was full, he would bless Esau.

That's how they rolled in biblical times. No need for wills or legal documents. They bestowed birthrights and such by simply patting you on the tippy top of your head (after consuming a whole animal).

Like the good son that he was, Esau went deer hunting.

Now, Rebekah overheard this convo (probably because she was eavesdropping, but we don't have any actual proof). And since she favored Jacob, she figured *he* should be the one to get their father's blessing.

While Esau was off hunting, Rebekah tells Jacob to grab one of the nearest kids. (No, silly. Not a *human* kid. A young, tender goat.) Since she was his wife, Rebekah also knew how to make the dish Papa Isaac was salivating for. Oh, the plot thickens.

The food situation was covered, but there was just one problem. Esau was a hairy dude. I mean Geico Caveman hairy. Isaac may have been old and blind but he was not a fool. Jacob and his mom figured Isaac would want to make sure he was blessing the right son and would run his fingers over Esau's hairy body. So, they improvised. First, Rebekah grabbed some of Esau's clothes for Jacob to wear so he could smell like him (Ew!). Then she took old goat skins and placed them on Jacob's skin, and voilà—instant body hair.

Isaac goes on to bless Jacob just as Esau returns from his hunt.

Cue the Law & Order sound effect.

Esau was outraged and threatened to off his brother, but Rebekah jumped in to help Jacob escape. She sent him to a land far, far away to live with his uncle. It was 20 years before the brothers met again. Fortunately, no blood was shed—and no one's credit score was damaged either.

Fast forward a few centuries. During these times, most crooks didn't steal your identity to fatten their wallets. They assumed another identity to escape from debt or hide from authorities or other criminals. These outlaws usually were simply trying to start a new life with a new persona.

Keep moving forward in history until 1984. You may have learned in history class that the United States banned the manufacture and sale of alcohol in 1920. This was known as *prohibition* because it forbade, or prohibited, people from getting their drink on. Prohibition lasted until 1933, when it was repealed by the 21st Amendment. Once again, people could drink legally.

Where was I? Right, 1984 (thanks for paying attention). In 1984, the U.S. Congress passed the National Minimum Drinking Age Act. Before that, each state had decided the legal drinking age for residents. But then someone decided the legal drinking age should be the same for everyone.

Now, I'm not exactly sure who decided "21" was the magical age when a person was suddenly mature enough to drink responsibly. Maybe someone was a fan of Fibonacci and recommended they choose the first reasonable number in the sequence (0, 1, 1, 2, 3, 5, 8, 13, 21, 34...). Some goofball probably initially voted for "13," but *that* was quickly overruled. Thirty-four was too old, of course. Or maybe someone was a fan of blackjack. Or, wait, here's a cool idea. Wait for it. Did you know that if you add:

$$1 + 2 + 3 + 4 + 5 + 6$$

you get—you guessed it (I hope)—21?

Or maybe it was random.

Whatever the reason, this new law threw a monkey wrench into the plans of many boozy college students. Before 1984, students living in states where they could not legally drink would simply cross state lines. Oh, they had a few other choices. They could hang out in front of a convenience store and ask an adult to buy alcohol for them. But no one wants to go to jail for contributing to the delinquency of a minor. Some probably begged older siblings, friends, or upper classmen to hook them up. The rest? I suppose they could make their own alcohol in the tub like they did during prohibition, but who wants to drink a beer that tastes like stinky feet?

They say that necessity is the mother of invention. Well, a 60-watt bulb went off in some budding entrepreneur's head. Before you could say "lite beer," the fake ID (a form of identity theft) was born.

Then things got real serious real quick because that's when people started using credit cards more often. Credit cards have been around for a long time. The idea was first proposed in the late 1800s. However, it wasn't until the 1930s that consumers started saying, "Put it on my card." Still, the average Joe (or Jill) did not have a credit card.

Since credit card use was limited, identity theft was pretty much non-existent. Many businesses allowed customers to open credit accounts. In fact, allowing customers to open a line of credit or run a "tab" had been a part of doing business for a long, long time. But generally the account information was kept in a ledger. You purchased something, it went in the ledger. You made a payment, yep, it went in the ledger. Some businesses issued store credit cards to customers, but these could only be used in their business, of course.

The next time you plunk down your (or your parents') credit card to pay for your "tall, non-fat latte with soy milk, extra whipped cream, and thinly drizzled caramel sauce," pause for a moment to give props to Mr. Frank McNamara.

Back in 1949, McNamara was dining with his lovely wife. When the check arrived:

"Ahem. Oh, dear," he blushed. "I seem to have forgotten my wallet."

Thankfully, his wife remembered her father telling her to always keep a few bucks in her purse (in case you have to ditch a sucker), so she was able to pay the bill. Frank was saved from the embarrassment of having to roll up his sleeves and wash dishes. Or even worse, they might have been forced to dine and dash.

From this embarrassment, McNamara, along with a partner, created a way for consumers to pay for a purchase without having cash on hand. In February 1950, he returned to that same restaurant. He didn't pay for his meal with cash this time; he paid for it with the Diner's Card, the first recognized consumer credit card. The Diner's Club became the first company to offer plastic to the general public. It wasn't actually plastic, it was cardboard, but you get the point. The card was mainly used to pay for dining and entertainment. A decade later, the plastic credit card made its debut.

Bank of America jumped on the bandwagon in 1966, issuing the BankAmericard, which would later morph into Visa. This was followed by MasterCard; and today, credit cards are offered by financial institutions up the wazoo.

Today, we think nothing of whipping out a credit card. But in its infancy, using a credit card was a pain. Before the 1980s, the store clerk had to first verify that your card was in good standing. They had to schlep a big binder full of account numbers onto the counter to make sure your card was legit. Or they would hold up the line calling the credit card company to verify your number.

So, as you can imagine, not a lot of people used credit cards. But those who did ran the risk of having their identities stolen. All a crook had to do was get their dirty little hands on the big book of account numbers—which could be found in major stores across the United States.

On a positive note, since the number of credit cards during this time was still pretty low, thieves were usually caught quickly. Good news for consumers—bad news for thieves.

Moving along to the swipe machines. Instead of binders full of account numbers or calls to the credit card company, a clerk could verify your card's status with a simple swipe. Can you guess what happened next? If you said "It became harder for thieves to steal credit card information," give yourself a gold star.

While this new technology made it harder, it did not make theft impossible. It simply meant the thieves had to work harder to get their hands on your money.

Finally, we end our journey in today's modern world. Unfortunately, it has become fairly easy for thieves to lift your personal information. Thanks, Internet! We have come a long way since the modem dial-up days of AOL (although I admit I kind of miss the ubiquitous, "You've Got Mail" greeting). Today we connect on laptops, desktops, smartphones, gaming systems, and more. I suspect in the near future we will connect to the Internet on any flat surface. Or even in the air.

With the mainstream popularity of the Internet, you can expect the number of identity theft cases to keep rising. Most of us make online purchases but never think about the safety of our financial information. Millions of people have had their identities stolen since credit cards were introduced.

But it is not just credit cards you need to worry about. Any type of personal information is fair game. This includes information you may not think would be useful, like your name, address, and date of birth. However, when this information is combined other vital information—like your Social Security number—a thief can be well on their way to causing you a lot of needless headaches.

WHO IS STEALING IDENTITIES?

Close your eyes for a moment. Picture in your mind the image of an identity thief. Go ahead, I'll wait.

You may have imagined a pimply-faced, 30-something nerd working frantically in his mom's basement. Or maybe you see Elliot, the socially awkward, hooded hacker from the TV show, *Mr. Robot*. The truth is, identity thieves look just like you and me. The person that scams you could be the cute barista at Starbucks or the emo chick sitting next to you on the bus. It could be your soccer coach or the secretary at your school.

Fast Fact

Identity thieves do not discriminate. They will steal your identity no matter your gender, race, or ethnicity. They don't care what state you live in or your economic status.

Many young people are the victims of "familial fraud" — most often a family member or close friend. If your identity is stolen, there's a good chance you may know the thief. You will learn more about familial fraud in Chapter 8, but for now you need to realize that it is easy for a family member or family friend to steal your identity. They will not have to resort to trickery, either. Instead, they can simply take your credit or debit card or your Social Security card.

Unfortunately, it is sometimes too tempting and too easy for people to steal your identity. This includes school and business employees that have access to your information. Thieves aren't always adults either. Recently, a 17-year-old McDonald's employee in Metairie, Louisiana, (a suburb outside of New Orleans) was arrested for taking photos of customers' credit and debit cards with her cellphone while working the drive-through window.[7] After her arrest, the employee admitted that she had been stealing information for two weeks. She used the stolen information to buy stuff off Amazon. This is not an isolated case; many cases of identity theft are inside jobs.

CELEBRITY VICTIMS

Let me stress again that no one is safe from identity theft. This includes celebrities. They don't live in protective bubbles, immune from life's everyday problems. Celebrities are people, and people fall victim to identity theft. Here are a few examples:

Tiger Woods: In 1998, Anthony Lemar Taylor used Woods' real name, Eldrick T. Woods, his Social Security number, and his date of birth to get a driver's license and credit card. Taylor went on a spending spree that lasted a year before he was caught. But not before he had spent $17,000. He was sentenced to the maximum 200 years in prison under California's three-strikes law.

Lily Allen: In 2008, the British pop star was surprised when she received a $7,000 bill from a cab company she had an account with. After further investigations, it was discovered that a stripper had gotten her hands on Lily's account information. The stripper then used the cab service to take her to and from work at the strip club.

7. Hunter, 2016

Will Smith: The Fresh Prince of Bel-Air was a victim of identity theft in 2002. Carlos Lomax used Smith's legal name—Willard C. Smith—to open 14 credit accounts in the singer/actor's name. Lomax charged over $30,000 before he was caught and sentenced to 37 months in prison.

When it comes to identity theft, no one can breathe easy. You can't cross your fingers and hope it won't happen to you. Neither should you get paranoid or avoid going online. Instead, you need to take the information from this book and put it to good use by following the steps outlined. In the next chapter, you will learn why people under 18 are often targets of identity theft.

CHAPTER 2

I'm Just a Kid. Who Would Want to Steal My Identity?

At this point you are probably wondering why anyone would want to steal your identity.

"I'm just a kid," you say. "I don't *have* a credit history."

It is this very reason identity thieves view children and young adults as attractive targets. Having a clean credit history makes it easy for a crook to get credit in your name. You have a spotless, unblemished record—until they stain it. Adults routinely check their credit reports. Teens—not so much. You probably will not realize someone has stolen your identity until you apply for your own credit years later. Or maybe when you apply for your first job.

Before we explore ways you protect yourself, let's take a moment to talk about what scammers do with your information once they get their hands on it.

WHAT DO THIEVES DO WITH YOUR INFORMATION AFTER IT'S STOLEN?

We have already established that most thieves don't want your identity so they can run off and start a new life under an assumed name. Once your identity is stolen, the thief will do one of two things: sell your information to someone else or use the information themselves.

In the first instance, the bandit is not looking for the long con. The name of the game in to get in and get out fast.

These con artists are known as "collectors." They are looking to make a quick buck. They collect your information — name, address, credit card information, Social Security number — and sell it to other people. They don't make money by selling just one person's information. Instead, they sell in bulk.

A report by SecureWorks revealed typical prices for various types of information. Here are a few examples:

Visa or MasterCard Number	$7.00
Email & Social Media Hacking	$129.00
Remote Access Trojans (RATs)	$40.00
Fullz (a file containing a person's name, Social Security number, birth date and other account numbers, and sensitive data)	$15–65[8]

Although these scammers may not make a lot of money selling one identity, they can make a comfortable living selling multiple identities or sensitive information each day. Think about it. If a scammer sells 10 fullz a day at $65 each, his profit is $650. That's $3,250 for a five-day work week. One hundred sixty-nine thousand dollars a year is a nice salary.

Even at $15 a pop, the collector can make $750 a week (selling 10 each day). I'm giving you conservative figures. Collectors can definitely make more depending on the type of information they have and how much they are able to sell.

The opposite of the collector is the "end user." This joker either personally steals your information or buys it from someone who has stolen it (the collector). The end user wants your information for his personal gain. For example, to open a new account or take out a loan.

In either scenario, once these criminals have your information, they can use it in several ways. Here are a few examples:

- You pay for your dinner with a credit card. The waiter swipes your card through a small device that records your information. He does this with several other patrons and then sells the information in bulk.

- You lose your wallet at the mall. Unfortunately, it has your Social Security card inside. Someone finds it, but instead of turning in to the lost and found, they use it to help a friend get a job and apartment in your name.

- You leave your computer unattended for just a second at a busy coffeehouse. When you turn around, someone has tiptoed off with it. This cat burglar is able to retrieve a file you thought was long deleted. The file has the password to your online bank account—which he proceeds to drain.

- You sign up for the neighborhood soccer league and the coach says he needs your Social Security number for insurance reasons. You think nothing of it, fill out the form like the rest of the team, and hand it over to your coach. The coach files all the forms in his home office. Your coach's brother is having some "issues." He sneaks into the office and picks a random form. He assumes your identity to open bank accounts, take out loans, and avoid the police.

- Someone steals your Social Security number and uses it to get a driver's license. Later, he's arrested and released on bail. Once released, he slinks out of town. A warrant is issued for his arrest. Through a bit of detective work, the crook's address is located. You open your door to the police, who are there to take you to jail. Thankfully, you prove that you are not the culprit. Eventually.

These examples highlight just a few of the many ways your information can fall into the wrong hands.

A CLOSER LOOK AT COLLECTORS

One of the reasons collectors are so willing to risk getting caught is the penalty. In many cases, they will receive the equivalent of a slap on the hand. State laws vary, but a first offender with a misdemeanor charge will typically get away with only having to pay a fine.

They may have to make restitution—repay the victims—but in most cases, they will not see the inside of a jail. A repeat offender or a thief charged with a felony may receive a jail sentence (in addition to paying fines and making restitution), but again, the amount of time served is usually fairly short in comparison to other crimes.

The risk of getting caught is low because these slippery scammers are usually able to cover their tracks. Collectors and end users employ tactics like IP address and phone spoofing to hide their real location. You will learn more about these tactics in the next chapter. But for now, realize these crooks are masters at hiding their digital footprint.

HOW THE END USERS USE YOUR IDENTITY

The collector has done his part. He stole your information and then sold it to make a quick buck. Your information may have passed through several hands before ultimately landing in the hands of the end user. Or maybe the end user stole the information himself. Either way, here is where the real damage begins. The end user will now use your information mainly for financial gain. Of course, there are other reasons, which we will also cover in this chapter.

Let's first look at the financial rewards of identity theft.

Opening a new account

The first thing an end user may do with your information is open a new credit card account or take out a loan in your name. They typically will open as many accounts as quickly as possible and then drain the funds.

Fast Fact

Even with a credit limit of $2,000, if a crook opens five new accounts, he can make $10,000 quickly from one stolen identity. Unless you receive a bill, it may take months or years before you realize your identity has been stolen.

To make matters worse, it's easy for a thief to use a credit card without providing any identification. In the early days, cashiers would check your identification, plus the signature on the back of the card. Not so much today. Unless you are purchasing an age-restricted product—like alcohol or cigarettes—the cashier barely gives you a second look when you whip out the plastic. Self-swiping machines also make it easy for crooks. In most cases, the cashier never has physical custody of your card.

Not to mention that the conveniences that make our lives easier also make it easier for crooks to use stolen cards. For instance, they can fill their car (and their thieving buddies' cars) with gas. All they need to do is drive up to the pump, swipe, and fill 'er up. No need to sign the receipt or show identification.

With the right amount of tools—a fake ID for example—an identity thief can take out a loan or open a bank account (where they can stash their stolen loot) in your name. Not all thieves open new accounts and run with the money. Some will need to use your identity longer and will actually pay the bills on time.

A typical case would involve someone with bad credit. They may use your identity to open an account. Let's say, a utility account, at their new apartment (which they have also rented using your identity). Since they need the utilities, they will pay on the account. Or maybe they bought a new cellphone in your name. Again, since they are using the cellphone, they will make the payments—at least until they no longer need it.

Cleaning out existing accounts

Some people mistakenly think that as long as a crook doesn't have physical custody of their credit or debit card, they are safe. As I have shown you previously (remember the McDonald's worker?), if a thief has your credit card number, the expiration date, and the security number (found on the back of the card), they can use your card to make online purchases. They can also use this information to make telephone purchases.

In Chapter 3, you will learn how scammers use spoofing, phishing, hacking, and other methods to steal your money. For now, just know that these crooks try really hard to trick you into giving up information that will give them access to your account. Typically, a screen name and password may be all they need.

Once they have access, they can drain your account *and* close it. Now your money's gone *and* your account is closed. Proving that you did not close the account—and withdraw the money—is usually difficult, if not impossible.

The problem with finding out who scammed you is also stalled by the way that thieves operate. They use public computers so that authorities cannot track their IP address. Or they use spoofing software to hide their IP address. How many times have you watched a TV show or movie where the police or FBI tracked an IP address to a certain location of the "bad guy," only to kick in the door of an 80-year-old grandmother?

With a fake ID, a thief can rent a P.O. Box and use it to receive ill-gotten items. Boxes are rented on an annual (yearly) or semi-annual (every six months) basis. Since boxes are relatively cheap, scammers have no qualms renting boxes in multiple locations. They can rent the boxes concurrently, or open an account, and get a bunch of stuff sent to them. Then never use that box again. They will simply keep opening and closing boxes as they order items bought using your identity.

Unfortunately for the victim, the thieves are able to cover their tracks. Detection is almost impossible because of these methods (spoofing, constantly moving money from account to account, etc.). Sadly, eventually the police will hit a brick wall. Your case will grow cold.

To the victim, a loss of even a few thousand dollars could be financially devastating, but it will not be enough to justify the police remaining involved when there are more pressing crimes that demand their focus.

NON-FINANCIAL WAYS IDENTITY THIEVES CAN RUIN YOUR LIFE

We have looked at ways the financial ways identity thieves can mess up your life. There are times, however, when they can cause trouble for you that does not involve money. One example is a sort of "get out of jail free card" for the crook.

Some crooks involved in illegal dealings often have fake documentation in case they are arrested. Let's look at one scenario:

Tom is a drug dealer. He purchased a fullz package from a scammer. He has a fake driver's license that he was able to get in your name using your Social Security number. He gets pulled over for speeding and the police find a stash of illegal drugs in his possession. His car is registered in his fake name. Everything about him is fake. Except the drugs. Although Tom is arrested, he is able to post bail because the amount of drugs is not substantial. He is released from jail quickly.

Out on bail, Tom quietly disappears. Maybe he has another identity already on hand or he has contacted a collector to secure a new one. Either way, "Tom" has a court appearance date, penciled in on the docket. What do you think will happen when that date arrives? I'll give you a moment to think.

You guessed it. "Tom" is in the wind, gone, vanished, missing in action. You get the picture. And you are temporarily left holding the bag for Tom's misdeeds.

Using Tom's Social Security information, police are able to track down Tom. But Tom is not the 35-year-old male previously arrested, but a 17-year-old with no idea that his identity has been stolen.

Will the police simply say, "My bad"? Um, no. It is possible that you will get arrested and have to prove that you're not the person who was originally charged.

Proving your innocence could be as easy as comparing your never-been-in-trouble-with-the-law face with Tom's mug shot taken on the night he was arrested. If you are unlucky enough to have even the slightest resemblance to Tom, proving it wasn't you that was arrested can cause even more of a headache.

You may have to provide an alibi for the night of the arrest. You may have to appear in court with the arresting officer for a positive identification. Hopefully, the officer will be able to positively say that you're not the "Tom" he arrested. Unfortunately, in large cities, police routinely arrest dozens of people each night. He may have trouble positively identifying you as the victim—and not the criminal—without corroborating evidence.

Another growing problem is the use of stolen identification for immigration purposes. Many people move to the United States from other countries and go through the proper steps required to become citizens. However, there are thousands of illegal immigrants currently in the United States—and more arrive daily.

Once in this country, illegal immigrants run the risk of being deported (sent back to their country) if they do not have proper documentation. Without proper documentation, these immigrants cannot legally work, rent a place to live, or get a driver's license.

One answer to their dilemma is to get their hands on a Social Security number. With one, they can get fake a ID and, most importantly, a job.

Because an illegal immigrant's main goal is to stay under the radar, you may never know that someone is using your identity—unless there is a serious problem. Illegal immigrants typically do not open credit accounts or take out loans; they simply want to work. So even if you check your credit report, you probably would not notice anything fishy.

It is also possible that an illegal immigrant will not actually steal your Social Security number. Have you ever noticed a car's license plate and realized it spelled a word but was not a vanity plate? With all of the possible permutations and combinations, you know eventually a random word is going to pop up. This is exactly what happens with illegal immigrants sometimes. They may apply for a job and make up a Social Security number. Totally random but, unfortunately for you, the number is your Social Security number.

Making this situation worse, many employers never check to see if an employee's Social Security number is valid. Illegal immigrants want to work and they will work a lot cheaper than most U.S. citizens. Employers realize this and are willing to look the other way.

If an illegal immigrant can get their hands on your Social Security number when you are an infant, they can have many, many years going about their business before you realize something is rotten. At that point, they can just buy another identity.

Scary stuff, right? I know the information I am giving you is troubling, but I swear there's good news. By the time you finish this book, you are going to be one bad, identity-thief-thwarting teen. Let's take a look now at how thieves steal your information.

CHAPTER 3

How Can Scammers Steal My Identity Online?

There are literally dozens of ways scammers can steal your identity. Right now as you sit reading this awesome book, arming yourself with the tools you need to protect yourself, criminals are hard at work thinking of new ways to scam you.

Before we look at actual ways your identity can be stolen, let's look at three types of personal information thieves are particularly interested in swiping.

HOT COMMODITIES

Social Security number: You probably know by now that one of the hottest commodities thieves want is your Social Security number. Fortunately, most people realize this, which is why we only release this nine-digit number to people who have a legitimate reason to request it.

This includes banks, schools, and credit card companies. You can always refuse to give out your number if you have concerns. Realize, though, that the person requesting the information can refuse to provide you with goods or services. Unfortunately, sometimes the people making the request are the ones stealing your identity.

If an identity thief has your Social Security number, it's like they won the lottery. They can use it to open new credit or bank accounts, get a job, a driver's license, and more.

If you have concerns, it is okay to ask why your number is needed, how it will be used, and who will have access to it. If the number is stored in a database, you want to know exactly how it will be displayed. For instance, some databases will block out most of your Social Security number with the exception of the last four digits. Only a few people will have access to the complete number. So a crook (including employees) accessing the database will see something like this:

xxx-xx-6789—which, in most cases, is completely useless.

The reason I say this information is useless "in most cases" is because there are times when you may need to only verify the last four digits of your Social Security number. This is generally done in addition to other information such as your date of birth. So, if a criminal knows a lot about you, they could possibly use this information.

Bank Account Personal Identification Number (PIN): Another sizzling hot commodity is your bank account's Personal Identification Number (PIN). If a thief has your card *and* your PIN—*cha-ching*—your money is ripe for the picking.

When you open a new account, the bank will not send your new card and PIN number at the same time. If they did, a mailbox thief could grab your card and PIN, activate your card, and use it before you are even aware the card is missing. That is why banks take this extra measure to ensure your account is not compromised.

Passwords: I don't know about you, but I have a ton of passwords for my various accounts. And I'm forgetful, so I write my passwords down. But I don't recommend you do the same unless you take added precautions.

If you *have* to write your passwords down, I suggest you create a system where you can identify the account, but no one else can. If someone finds my list of passwords, it would be useless unless they are somehow able to crawl inside my head and figure out how my brain works. Trust me, that is not an easy task.

Of course, I do not have the list in electronic format, so there is no chance of someone finding the list on my computer. But someone could find the hand-written copy. But again, it will look like a bunch of gibberish. They probably will not even realize it is a list of passwords (it's not like I wrote **PASSWORDS** across the page).

One way to stop criminals is to change your passwords often. Also, make sure you do not use the same password for multiple accounts. This is crucial. Scammers are smart and realize that humans like to make things easy for themselves. This includes using the same password for multiple accounts. So, if a thief has the password for one account and knows about your other accounts, he or she will usually try the known password first.

It's not only financial accounts you need worry about. Hacking email accounts is big business for thieves. Recently, Yahoo confirmed that in 2014, as many as 500 million users' accounts may have been compromised.[9] 500 million! Hackers gained access to sensitive data including names, email addresses, telephone numbers, and dates of birth.

Reportedly, financial information—like banking information—was stored in a different system and, according to Yahoo, was not affected. However, users were urged to change their passwords. Especially vulnerable were users who had not changed their password in the last two years. But think about it, hackers had users' information for two years. Two years! Can you imagine what type of damage may have been done during that time?

Fast Fact

How would having access to your email password help scammers? Good question. A scammer can claim they have lost their password. Requesting a password reset usually involves sending a link to the email address associated with your account. The scammer can then reset your password—locking you out of your own account.

Your email may contain information that thieves can use, such as your phone number. Along with your information, they will also have access to your contacts' information. And, of course, they can read all of your current, saved, and outgoing messages, too.

9. Lord, 2016

Basically, whatever information is in your inbox, the crooks will have access to and can use in ways we can't even begin to imagine, because we are honest folk.

In conjunction with these three pieces of information, if a scammer has additional data, like your driver's license number and date of birth, there is no telling the amount of damage they can cause. Now, let's take a look at ways scammers get your information.

HACKING

I remember when I first heard about hackers. I thought they were cool. I secretly wanted to be a hacker. Why not? A hacker was not a malicious crook. Curious, yes; mischievous at best. No way were these nerds criminals, I thought.

Early hackers had one goal in mind — gain access to a computer's system. Once inside, they could poke around. Then they could back flip out before anyone noticed what was happening. Most of the hacking was aimed at governmental departments or big businesses. Hacking a supposedly un-hackable system *and* outsmarting adults was all a game to many hackers. Most never caused any real damage.

Okay, a few hackers might perform (what they considered) harmless tricks. They might change a grade, for example. But even in this case, they might change the grade for someone else — someone who did not even ask them. For example, if a hacker had a crush on a particular girl, he might change a grade just to see her smile.

Today, hacking is a serious menace. Although there are still hackers that aren't malicious, many more use their skills to commit crimes, including identity theft.

What exactly is "hacking"? Cyber.laws.com, defines hacking as "Modifying or altering computer software and hardware to accomplish a goal that is considered to be outside of the creator's original objective." So, basically, hacking involves someone gaining access to your computer, without your permission, with the goal of somehow causing you harm.

Although hacking is harmful to the person or entity that has been hacked, it is considered a "white-collar crime." The Federal Bureau of Investigation (FBI) reports that the term was first coined in 1939 and refers to crimes usually "characterized by deceit, concealment, or violation of trust and are not dependent on the application or threat of physical force or violence."[10]

It is because of this reason — lack of physical violence — that many refer to these attacks as "victimless crimes." Of course, we know that's not true. A victim of identity theft can have their lives turned upside down. Although no physical assault took place, the damage is just as severe.

10. Federal Bureau of Investigations

Anti-virus software giant, McAfee, estimates that the cost of cybercrime to individuals and businesses is \$375 to \$500 billion annually.[11] Even if a hacker does not try to steal your identity—let's just say a hacker is upset with you and hacks your computer to post unflattering pictures of you to your social media accounts—he has flung open the door for a criminal to easily walk through. Whenever someone hacks your computer, your system becomes vulnerable and an easy target for other criminals.

GAINING ACCESS BY USING THE BACKDOOR

Like many crooks, hackers creep through the backdoor to get your stuff. A backdoor—sometimes called a trapdoor—is a way to bypass the authentication process in order to access a software program or computer. Most computer programs have built-in backdoors. Here's why.

As humans, we often forget things (our passwords, for example). If the program you are trying to access does not have a way to email your password to you, then the next step would be to contact the company to regain access. This is where backdoors come in.

You see, companies know that we are forgetful, so they have already prepared for your call by installing a way to bypass the login information—the backdoor. A backdoor can help you regain access to your computer or software program, but this also makes it easy for a hacker to gain backdoor access and steal your identity.

If a hacker is able to get into your computer using the backdoor, he can cause all kinds of trouble, like installing malicious software or gaining remote access to your computer.

11. McAfee, 2014

CRACKING YOUR PASSWORD CODE

Another way for hackers to access your account is by cracking your pass-words. As added security, sometimes the password requirements may seem a bit . . . much. The password for one of my accounts must be *exactly* fif-teen characters long (plus other requirements). I have another account that will not accept a password with repeating letters or numbers. And I don't mean appearing consecutive—as in bu<u>bb</u>le, or 4<u>55</u>9. No, I mean you can only use the letter "b" or the number "9" once.

Just remember, as annoying as some of the requirements may seem, these measurements have been put in place for your safety. Unfortunately, even with added levels of security, a hacker can figure out your password. Some-times without breaking a sweat.

There are programs that actually help hackers figure out your password. Let me introduce you to a couple of them.

- **The Dictionary Attack:** Suppose you could figure out a person's password by entering every single word in the dictionary. That is exactly how the dictionary attack works. These assaults are sometimes called brute force attacks.

   Hackers count on people using simple passwords. Using this type of software, a hacker can sit back and let the program do all of the dirty work. These programs only work on sites that do not require users to choose alpha-numeric passwords or special characters (!, &, *, etc.).

   What should you do if a site does not have a stringent password requirement policy? Suppose you can get by with simply entering any eight-letter word? Should you pick a common word? The answer, of course, is no.

   You can still stop a hacker by using a word that is not commonly found in the dictionary. Or go ahead and make up a word. Regardless of the site's requirements, I almost always make up words when creating passwords.

- **The Hybrid Attack:** Hackers are always trying to stay one step ahead of the game. They have no intention of letting a little thing like special characters stop them from figuring out your password. Instead, for sites that require users to create a password that uses both numbers and/or special characters, hackers will hit you with a counterpunch—the hybrid attack. These programs check for both simple words *and* add-ons. The premise is the same though. The hacker runs the program, then sits on his duff until a match is found.

BLOCKING HACKERS

To fight back against both types of attacks, many sites have added measures to thwart hackers. Have you ever typed in a password and received an "incorrect" error message? If you continue to type in the incorrect password, you may get locked out after 3–5 tries.

At this point, a few things can happen. You may get locked out for a certain amount of time (usually 15–30 minutes). After this time has passed, you can try to sign in again. If you legitimately made a mistake, after the time has lapsed you should be able to sign in — no harm, no foul. But a computer program will continue to get locked out, unless it cracks the password.

Some sites may lock you out and instruct you to call customer support before you can access your account. Since these programs can't make phone calls and carry on human-type conversations, they are locked out once again.

Some sites will lock you out and automatically send a password reset link to the email address associated with your account. And unless a hacker has already hacked into your email, you're covered. Plus, you're tipped off. This happened to me with an email account that I don't use often. Someone tried to hack it but was locked out. I received a password reset email and immediately contacted the help desk to let them know that someone was trying to hack my account.

You may have also tried logging into a site that uses CAPTCHA verification — Completely Automated Public Turing Test To Tell Computers and Humans Apart. You know what I'm talking about, right? In case you don't, let me explain.

You know that weird little box on a website that instructs you to type in the information you see? That's CAPTCHA. Even with my glasses on, sometimes the information is so blurry and wavy, I can barely read it. That, my friend, is the point. A human (eventually) will figure out the (blurry) information. However, malicious software won't.

I have also noticed that some sites added an extra layer of protection. After you enter the CAPTCHA information, you will also have to check a box verifying: "I am not a robot." But wait, there's more. You have to select particular images from a group of pictures. For example, they may ask you to select all images that are cats, boats, ice cream, etc.

So, it seems like it would be hard for a hacker to get to your goodies. When professional hackers run into a wall, they find a way to jump over it. And unless the wall goes straight up to heaven, they will find a way to gain access to your account.

One way crooks can get your password is by skipping over you altogether. Instead, they hack the database containing users' passwords. This is what happened in the Yahoo breach mentioned previously. That's why it's a good reason to change your passwords often.

TYPES OF HACKERS

But not all hackers are bad. The government and companies hire hackers as security consultants. Hackers may test a network's security to look for vulnerabilities, for example. The ability to hack a system is not a crime. Using your skills for malicious reasons, however, is. There are actually different classifications of hackers:

- **White hat hackers:** These are the good guys. They work with companies to identity security weaknesses. They may also work with the government to help catch criminals.

- **Black hat hackers:** On the flip side of the coin, we have the bad guys. Black hats' hack attacks (whoa, try to say that three times) are always malicious. The twist is they may not use the attack to steal your identity or for financial gain. They may instead pinch secret government documents. They often believe that they are doing a good deed by, for example, releasing a (perceived) corrupt politician's personal email or a business cover-up. The bottom line is, whenever you illegally access someone's personal information, you are committing a crime.

- **Gray hat hackers:** Dangling in the middle between the good and bad guys are the gray hats. They may use their skills, for instance, to expose a company's network vulnerabilities. That makes them good guys, or white hats. Then, they turn to the dark side by contacting the company to ask for money to fix the problem. If they don't pay up, the hackers could threaten to take advantage of what they discovered.

- **Blue hat hackers:** Before a company launches a program, they need to make sure there aren't any holes that need patching. Although they may have their own white hat team, they will look outside the company and hire someone on a freelance basis to test the program before it launches. Most of these hackers are good guys. However, for some, the temptation to exploit what they've found is too hard to resist. They may then slip into the gray hat category or use what they have discovered for other nefarious reasons.

- **Script Kiddies:** These hackers do not have the skill set or experience to hack without assistance. But they can follow directions or a script.

They get the instructions from more experienced hackers—which they can easily find online in hacker forums and message boards. Then these junior hackers perform the steps outlined for them in black and white.

If there is an upside to this type of hacking, it is this: Since script kiddies do not have the brains to figure out what to do if they encounter a problem that's not outlined in the instructions, they will not be able to steal your identity. When they get stuck and can't figure out what to do next, they usually give up.

MALWARE

You probably have an anti-virus program installed on your computer. The program sits quietly in the background as you go about your daily Internet activities. Like a Marvel superhero, it protects you from would-be attackers by blocking potential threats.

On the program's radar is a particular nasty brand of software known as "malware." Malware stands for malicious software and includes spyware, adware, and other programs that can steal your identity. If you don't have anti-virus software installed, you may not be aware that you have malware on your computer because the bug is attached to other programs you have downloaded (and assumed were safe). Unfortunately, the hidden malware is far from innocent and can cause headaches for you.

A popular type of malware is one everyone has heard of, a virus. Once a virus runs amok on your system, it can delete files, reformat your hard drive, and perform other disgusting tricks. But it does not stop there. You can catch one of these little bugs by downloading files, games, etc. from the Internet. Viruses are especially troublesome because they can easily spread between computers.

Ah, cookies. Normally, I get so excited when I hear someone mention cookies. My favorite cookie is the Pepperidge Farms milk chocolate macadamia. I'm eating one right now even as I write this book. But there is another type of cookie—and it doesn't taste half as good.

I am referring to tracking cookies. When in the wrong hands, these cookies can lead to identity theft. Many websites use cookies to track information about visitors. This could include your shopping preferences or your financial information. Many sites alert visitors that they use cookies, but some do not. A cookie is simply a text file stored on your computer. These cookies are potential goldmines for hackers because the tracking software can supply them with the information they need to steal your identity.

Let's take a closer look at two vicious types of malware.

Spyware: This software does exactly what it sounds like—it tracks or spies on you, collecting information that is then sent to a third party. Spyware will track your movements, including your browsing history. Some types of spyware can even change your home page without your consent or keep opening your browser to sites you did not request.

Have you heard of free TV and movie streaming sites? These sites are notorious for picking up malware. I know it sounds like a good deal. Why pay for a streaming service when you can get it for free? Believe me, you will be better off paying the few dollars for Hulu, Netflix, or Amazon Video, rather than taking the chance of losing your identity (or money) when malware is loaded onto your computer.

Spyware also comes attached to programs you knowingly download and trust. You probably will not know if you have spyware on your computer unless an anti-virus program identifies it. Otherwise, you will have to look in your "add and delete" program files and manually uninstall it. Unfortunately, some spyware is hard to locate; you might need to install extra programs to find it.

You may wonder how a crook can use spyware to steal your identity. Let me tell you how—keystrokes. Spyware comes bundled with programs you download and, most importantly, trust. If your computer is not protected, you can unknowingly expose personal information.

Let's say, for example, you are bored and decide to head over to Steam to download a new game.

"Wow, *Teenage Mutant Zombie-Eating Turtles.* Sounds interesting," you think.

Since it's free, you download the game and play into the wee hours of the morning. What you don't know, however, is keystroke (also referred to as keylogging) spyware was also downloaded and installed on your computer. How does that help an identity thief?

The identity thief can see every key you tap. This information can easily help these scoundrels figure out your login information.

Let's say someone is tracking you and they see you hit:

$$w - w - w - . - g - o - o - g - l - e - . - c - o - m - enter,$$

then sees you tap,

$$y - o - u - r - n - a - m - e - 1 - 9 - enter,$$

he can guess that you have just signed into your email. He also knows that the next keys you enter will be your password. The same goes for financial accounts such as your bank's website or PayPal.

Adware: Similar to spyware because it tracks your Internet footprint, adware is a form of advertising that pops up when you are online. However, unlike spyware, a user may agree to use the software, even though it comes embedded with adware. Why? It is a way for a user to get free software. In exchange, they agree to accept advertising.

Initially, adware was not a bad trade off. Users received free software. The advertisements were targeted so the user might actually have an interest in what the ads were selling. Not all adware embedded in software is malicious, but a bunch of it is. Scammers see this as a quick and easy way to collect your personal information — and ultimately to steal your identity.

YOU'VE GOT (SPAM) MAIL

There are days when I dread checking my email. The reason? Spam — unsolicited (and annoying) junk messages. Not a day goes by when my inbox is not flooded with this waste of gigabytes. *Click. Click. Click.* That's the sound of me clicking away as I delete spam. How much spam do you receive in a day?

Probably a lot. In the 2016 Internet Security Threat Report (released by security provider Symantec), it was estimated that in 2015 a whopping 190 billion emails were sent every day. Of that number, 53 percent was spam and one out of every 1,846 spam messages was a phishing excursion.[12]

Not only is spam annoying, but if you are not careful, a scammer could claim you as his next victim. How? I am so glad you asked. Spammers often tout wonderful, amazing—and sometimes free—products.

Whatever they are selling, it sounds like a good deal, right? So you order one (or two), then sit back and wait for your product to arrive. Problem is the "product" does not exist. Or if it does, it is inferior to the advertised product. You have been duped. The scammer has your financial and other personal information. We have learned that scammers are good at covering their tracks, so good luck finding them.

---

12. Symantec, 2016

Here's an unedited example of a spam email straight from my inbox:

Compliment Your Fitness Efforts With Exclusive Weight Loss Product

Have you been dreaming of a beautiful body, but had no results with diets, workouts and supplements?

Our incredible solution with a breakthrough formula will deliver you the results you've been so eager to **achive**.

Click Here!

Powerful weight loss product that amplifies **methabolism**, stimulates positive mood and formulated for both men and women.

You can probably guess what would happen if you click on the link. Yep, you may unknowingly download malware. Even if the page looks legitimate, and you decide to order the product, you better believe you are going to get scammed.

Let me step back a minute. Did you notice anything odd about the two words in bold print? Yes, the scammer spelled achieve (**achive**) and metabolism (**methabolism**) incorrectly. Mistakes like this are often a clue that the email is bogus. But many people ignore the misspellings because they think they are about to get a good deal.

If you "buy" a product from a spammer, they will have your financial information, but that is not all. Remember, you are (supposedly) having the product(s) shipped to you, so the crook also has other vital information like your mailing address, email, and phone number.

If you fall for this scam, the bandit will not need physical custody of your credit card to use it. They have everything they need to make a purchase: your credit card number, expiration date, and security code.

"But what about free offers?" you ask. The same warning applies. First, the scammer does not have an actual product. Second, you may wonder why the company offering the product would request your credit card information if the offer is free. They often use the excuse that they need to verify that you are real or to prove where you live. If you are ever offered a free product but you have to pay some type of fee (including shipping and handling), the product is not actually free.

GONE PHISHING

One of the easiest ways for a scammer to steal your identity is when you willingly hand it over. They just love cooperative victims. You may have heard about phishing and spoofing but are not exactly sure what the terms mean. Let me explain. You may see the two terms used interchangeably, but spoofing and phishing are two different sides of the same bad coin. Scammers may use the methods in conjunction, however.

Dictionary.com defines phishing as, "The practice of using fraudulent emails and copies of legitimate websites to extract financial data from computer users for the purpose of identity theft."[13]

Spoofing, according to Dictionary.com, is "The act or an instance of impersonating another person on the Internet or via email."[14]

So, in simple terms, you can think of phishing as the way the crooks get your information, while spoofing is the way the hoax is delivered to you.

---

13. Dictionary.com, 2016
14. Dictionary.com, 2016

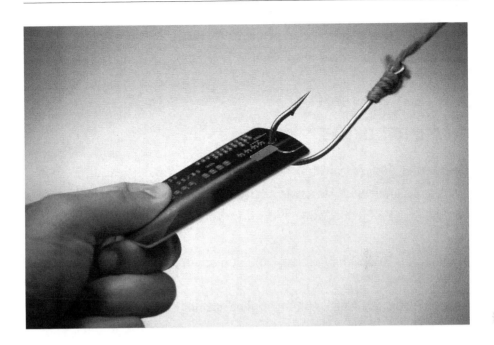

If you receive an email claiming to come from your bank (and it isn't), that's spoofing—the scammer's method of delivery. Let's pretend the email warned you that your account had been compromised. You are told to sign into your account to change your password. When you click on the included link, you are redirected to a website that looks identical to your bank's. Although the website may look like your bank's, it's not. When you log in, you have given the crooks your username and password. This retrieval of the information is phishing.

A scammer can also instruct you to download an attached file. Of course, the file contains a virus or some other malware, so definitely do not download it (or click on any links). This is an easier method than going through the trouble of setting up a fake website. However, more people are skeptical about downloading a file than they are of going to a website that they assume is legitimate.

The sad news is that millions of people fall for phishing and spoofing scams. But I am going to show you how you can avoid being in that number. Let's look at the two types of spoofing: email and website.

EMAIL SPOOFING

A scammer does his phishing without a rod or a reel. Instead, he uses a computer, along with dozens of email addresses. One of those addresses could be yours. Here's how the scammer will try to hook you.

You log in to your email account and you see this curious message:

Suspicious Activity On Your Online Account

The message appears to have originated from American Express:

amex@memberservice.com

This is an actual email I received. The problem is I don't have an American Express card, so I knew right away it was a scam. But this message is a good illustration of how email spoofing works. So let's continue.

The body of the message went a little something like this:

Dear Valued Card Member,

As part of American Express Online commitment to provide you with exceptional service, American Express Online is taking additional steps to ensure that your account data is secure.

We are sending you this email as a security notification, to confirm to you the inability to accurately verify your account information due to an internal error within our server.

You are required to review your account information **to prevent any future attention with your card online access.**

To get started, we have sent you an attached HTML Web Page.

See Attached for HTML Web Page

1- Download and Save it to Desktop
2- Go to Desktop to open the HTML Web Page-
3- Get Started by Filling your Information

Thank you for your continued Card membership.

Sincerely,
American Express Customer Care

If you are an American Express card member, you may not think twice about following these instructions. Okay, maybe this weird phrase: "**to prevent any future attention with your card online access,**" may have you a little confused. But many people will not hesitate to download the file—or, in this case, an actual webpage—and fill in the requested information.

Another message I received was also from "American Express"—these spammers really want me to have an Amex Card, apparently. In this message, they said my card was used to purchase $986 worth of loot on Amazon. This purchase "automatically triggered our fraud detection system," they claimed. As a result, the purchase was blocked and my account was frozen.

What do you think they instructed me to do next?

A) Call Amazon and give them a piece of my mind for allowing an unauthorized user to make purchases with my card.

B) Cancel my Amex Card and get a new one with a lower interest rate.

C) Verify my account information by downloading an attached file and proceed with the requested details.

If you answered "C," you have been paying attention. Give yourself a pat on the back.

You know the drill by now. If you download the file, you can count on downloading a malicious program. What I love most about this message is this final parting thought:

> "Please understand that this is our security measure intended to help and protect you and your account."

I love it when a spammer tries to pretend he is not a spammer by pretending he is concerned about the security of my account!

In a different email (yes, I get a lot of spam), this was attached:

> Note: We are not spammers and are against spamming of any kind. If you are not interested, then you can reply with a simple \"no\", we will never contact you again.

Should I respond? Nope. Never respond to a spam message. In this particular case, I knew it was both spam and a lie. Let me explain.

The gist of the message was: This dude was surfing the web when he came across my website, and "despite having a great design; it was not ranking on any of the search engines (Google Yahoo and Bing) for most of the keywords relating to your business."

Although I have a website, the email address the message was sent to is not affiliated with it. I use this address to get newsletters, information, etc., basically anytime I don't want to use my primary email. So, I knew he was full of crap.

Plus, my email address is not on my website. If you want to contact me, you do so by filling out a contact form. So, again, I knew he was lying. This email is another example of a phishing message, even though it does not ask me to click on a link or download a file. How? Good question. Here's how:

The sender claims that he can get my website to rank No. 1 on Google. All I have to do is give him 15 minutes of my time. Sounds good? Nope. The scammer is trying to do one of two things:

1. Scammers buy email address lists, but there is no guarantee how accurate the information is. So, they often attempt to verify that the email is active by asking you to respond to the email in some way. For example, they may ask you to unsubscribe from future mailings. A lot of people fall for this because they are trying to keep spam out of their inbox. Unsubscribing seems like a logical option. The problem is you end up getting more spam once your email address has been verified.

2. The scammer will try to reel you in by making promises; and if you take the bait, they will try to coax your personal information from you. In this example, if I agree to give him his 15 minutes, he would try to sell me his phony service. If I take the bait, I would hand over my credit or debit card information, including the expiration date and security code.

You should never, ever respond to spam. If the message has a "click here to unsubscribe" link, do not do it. If the message instructs you to reply to the message with "unsubscribe" or some other word(s) in the subject line, again, do not do it.

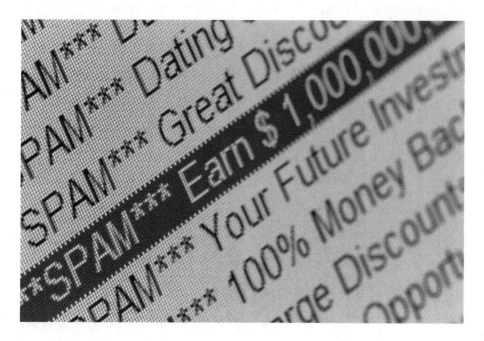

Are you familiar with the term "dumb criminal"? Well, there are dumb scammers, too. The previous examples illustrate examples of scammers who actually make an effort to pretend they are legitimate. Then you have these guys . . .

I recently received this message with the subject line:

Temporarily blocked

I knew it was spam, but since I was deep into writing this book, I opened the message hoping for material I could use. I was not disappointed. Here is the unedited message:

Dear myra,

this is to inform you that your Debit Card is temporarily blocked as there were unknown transactions made today.

We attached the scan of transactions. Please confirm whether you made these transactions.

King regards,
Lilia Barton
Technical Manager - Online Banking
email: Barton.79791@homegifts.ca

So many problems with this email. Let's start with the lowercase "m" in my name. Then move on to the bad grammar. These crooks could not bother to capitalize the first word of the badly-constructed sentence.

And did this wannabe thief just sign off with "King regards" instead of kind? I can't even. The thing that really makes me chuckle about this email is the spammer did not make any attempts to spoof the email address of a financial institution.

By the way, Mr. or Ms. Spammer, am I supposed to know which debit card you are referring to? Maybe I have multiple cards. But I digress. If you look at the email address, you will notice it's from **homegifts.ca**—not a bank or financial institution. This is another tell-tale sign.

I often receive messages, reportedly from a financial entity with a Gmail, Yahoo, or some obscure return email address. *Duh*—Chase, Visa, or MasterCard would never send an email from a non-domain account. But, unfortunately, some people still fall for scams like this because they do not look closely at the little details.

So, let's review to make sure we are still on the same page. In the examples above, the message from "American Express" is the spoof. The scammer is perpetrating a hoax by pretending they are calling from card member services. The phishing part of the scam is the attempt to extract information from me by downloading a webpage and file. Got it? Okay, let us move on then.

When you receive an email like the ones I mentioned, sometimes you go into panic mode. You may not stop to ask yourself if this is a scam or not. This is exactly what the scammers are counting on. If only a few take the bait, it can be financially rewarding for the scammers.

Instead of directing you to take care of this urgent issue, the scammer may tell you to call a number to verify your account. When you call the number, the scammer will answer. Or one of his buddies. Scammers get lonely, so they often work in groups.

The "customer service representative" will try to coax you into giving out your personal information. They may ask your password so they can reset it. They may ask for your Social Security number to verify you are who you say you are. Imagine that! You have to prove your identity to the scammer, who will then turn around and steal it.

The bottom line is this: if you think your account has been compromised, never click on a link, download a file, or call the number you are instructed to call. If you are told to call, make sure you call the number on the company's website. If you are told that your account has been frozen, go to the website (not from the link) and try to log on. If you can successfully log on, then you know someone was on a phishing expedition. Luckily, this book is teaching you how not to take the bait.

Some scammers will hold your personal information for days or even weeks before they actually use it. As discussed in Chapter 2, scammers may collect your information to sell, unless they are the end user. Either way, once they get your information, they can sit on it until they are ready to use it.

Please remember that scammers are after more than your financial accounts. Any online account you have is at risk. This includes your social media accounts and subscription accounts like Netflix, Hulu, and music streaming services. Ditto for gaming sites. Any account you have online is of interest to a phisher.

If they are able to access your account, then they can find out information about you that may not be readily available elsewhere. For example, in your Facebook or Twitter accounts, they will have access to sensitive information that may help in stealing your identity. Also, if you have your Facebook privacy settings to where only your friends can see your posts, once inside your account, a scammer may be able to find out the answers to typical account security questions. For example, your mother's maiden name, your father's middle name, the name of your first pet, your favorite teacher, and so on.

If someone accessed my Facebook account, they can also gain access to my private groups. Although they are mainly writing groups, I often post non-writing related personal information. Since the group is closed, I feel more comfortable posting information that I would never post publicly. If you have private groups, think of the type of personal information you post that could help a thief access your accounts.

Finally, criminals are willing to gamble that many people use the same passwords for their online accounts. If they have access to one, they can often gain access to others. This can lead to your financial accounts being hacked.

IP ADDRESS SPOOFING

One way scammers cover their tracks is by spoofing their Internet Protocol (IP) address. Crooks often use public computers to commit crimes. This makes it virtually impossible for authorities to trace the deed back to them. Others prefer to scam from the comfort of their own homes, using their own computers.

An IP address is a series of unique numbers used to identify a computer or other devices on a local or network Internet connection. When you send an email, the recipient can easily find your IP address by looking at the "full headers" in your message.

If a spammer sends messages from his own computer, the recipient can use an IP lookup site to find the IP address. This information is useful in helping authorities locate the sender. Computer-savvy scammers can wiggle around this issue by changing (spoofing) the IP address in their outgoing messages.

Most scammers have little fear of being caught. Even if authorities are able to locate these scam artists, many operate outside of the United States, so fear of legal prosecution is low.

WEBSITE SPOOFING

We have already discussed website spoofing as it relates to email phishing scams. Sometimes scammers will create a website to steal identities but it will not be part of a phishing expedition. The amount of time and effort the crook invests will determine the success of the con.

A less-experienced scammer may throw a website up quickly and hope for the best. Someone who wants to make sure he steals your identity will spend time creating a website that looks legitimate. They are looking for the big payoff. Investing weeks (months even) perfecting the scam is no biggie to them.

One of the biggest targets for scammers is the e-commerce website, PayPal. With a PayPal account, you can send and receive money without having to give out your bank information. However, if scammers access your account, they can make purchases or transfer money from your account to their own bank account. We have already learned that bank accounts can be faked. By the time authorities try to freeze the scammer's account, chances are good that the account is going to have a zero balance.

A 2013 report by software security vendor Trend Micro illustrates just how widespread the spoofing of PayPal's website is. According to the report, during the 2012 holiday season, scammers created 18,947 fake PayPal websites.[15] With the mad holiday rush, they probably banked (no pun intended) on shoppers being too rushed to notice if anything was "off."

So, how does the hoax work? If you receive a phishing message, the link will take you to a fake website. The scammer is counting on you not realizing the link doesn't take you to paypal.com (PayPal's official site). One way to make sure you are on the correct site is to check the URL in the address bar on your browser. If you see an address such as paypalsecure.com or paypal.us, back out as fast as you can.

If you do not, here is what will happen. If the scammer has done a good job, the website will look enough like PayPal to convince you to sign in. If you do, the thief will steal your credentials and, eventually, your money.

15. Pajares, 2013

These swindlers are clever, though. You will not even realize you have been scammed. After you log in, a pop-up screen will tell you that you have entered an incorrect password. Next, you will be redirected to the real Pay-Pal website.

After you successfully log in, you will think nothing of what happened. Who among us has not entered the wrong password? Good, no one raised their hand. We are all human and we make mistakes. Back to the scam.

You go on about your day, not knowing that a crook is about to steal your money or sell the information to another crook. Either way, unless you logged on to withdraw all of your funds *and* close your account, you can say bye-bye to your money.

There are other devious ways a scammer can trick you into giving out your login information. They purchase an internationalized domain name (IDN) similar to a popularly recognized domain. Unlike regular domain names, an IDN can contain script or alphabets from another language, like Chinese, Arabic, or French.

A scammer will purchase an IDN domain—pãypal.com, for example—and set up a fake website that mirrors the real PayPal. The spammer then goes phishing, warning that your account has been compromised. They provide a link (*ahhhh*, how nice) for you to log in to change your password. The link redirects you to pãypal.com, but you probably will not notice the tilde (the little squiggly line) over the first "a." So, you go ahead and log in. Once again, the crook has your information.

Scammers have also found an easy way to spoof websites by purchasing domains containing English letters that look similar.

Here is a good example. You have an account with **1stCreditBank.com**. Did you know that the lower-case "L" looks a lot like the number "1"? Here's a pop quiz. Which of these is the number 1? Don't peek at the answer.

1) l

2) 1

Okay, how did you do? If you guessed #1 was is the number 1, you are, drum roll . . . *wrong*. Number 1 is actually a lower-case "L." As you can see, it is impossible to tell the two apart. So if a spammer bought the IDN domain lstCreditBank.com (that's a lower-case "L") and a phishing message redirected you to the website, you would not be able to tell that you weren't at 1stCreditBank.com (the actual site). The English keyboard has other characters that look similar. Zero and capital "O", for example.

BOTS

Everything I know about robots I learned from science fiction writer Isaac Asimov. The first of Asimov's *Three Laws of Robotics*, states:

> A robot may not injure a human being or, through inaction, allow a human being to come to harm.[16]

Apparently, some robots did not get the memo. Computer robots—or bots, for short—are a particularly grotty type of malicious software hackers use to wreak havoc, including stealing your identity. If your computer becomes infected with a bot it does not work alone. Instead, it is part of a bot network (botnet), controlled by a "master." These networks can contain a *bazillion* infected computers. Okay, maybe not a *bazillion* but thousands, and in some cases, tens of thousands.

16. Jiyon, 2016

A master can program a bot to perform a variety of tasks, including sending spam. Bots are also known for distributed denial of service (DDoS) attacks, known for crashing entire websites. Once a site is down, the hacker may blackmail the owner by refusing to stop the attacks until they pay up. Not wanting to lose business, the company often has no choice but to pay the ransom.

Of course, bots are used by hackers to steal passwords and other sensitive data. What makes bots attractive to cybercriminals is the lightning fast speed at which they are able to perform these mundane tasks. Let's take a closer look at how botnets work.

Bots search the Internet looking for venerable computers to infect. When one is located, the bot slips in, infects the system, then reports back to the master. Infected machines are called "zombies," because once the bot is inside, it waits quietly until the master wakes it up by issuing a command to perform a task.

Fast Fact

A bot can enter your system in many different ways. For example, you can unknowingly download a bot from a website, or a bot can arrive in your inbox from another infected computer.

Here's what is interesting yet scary about botnets. As I mentioned, bots work in concert with other bots to form a network. So, if your infected computer is part of a network, you will unwittingly take part in criminal activities. Plus—listen to this—the person who infected your computer makes money by renting your computer to other criminals!

Imagine if someone rented out your house during the day while you were at school and your parents were at work. Of course, they leave before everyone returns. But that would be crazy right? Well, that's how crazy this situation is.

Bots are so adept at hiding and covering their tracks that you may not know your computer is infected. Security giant Norton warns that you may not know your computer is infected until you are contacted by your Internet Service Provider (ISP) for sending spam.[17] If you notice that your computer is running sluggish, this could be a sign that you have a bot. Not necessarily, because computers do run slow at times, but better safe than sorry. So, check your system out.

TYPOSQUATTING

Have you ever mistakenly typed the wrong URL into your browser? Most of us have. Typosquatting (also called URL hijacking) allows hackers to take advantage of human typographical errors.

17. Norton

Typosquatters purchase domain names that are eerily similar to well-known brands. For example, Goggle.com, CapitolOne.com, or facelook.com. They may also add a "." to the domain name, such as you.tube.com. As with website spoofing, hackers often create an identical site aimed at one thing: stealing your identity.

Hackers use typosquatting to trick you into handing over personal information much in the same ways already discussed. They may also use a particularly venomous method known as drive-by downloads.

DRIVE-BY DOWNLOADS

By now you know how important it is to think before you click on a link or download software. You also know that sometimes, despite your best efforts, your computer may get infected by a bot or malware bundled with software you trust.

Now, let's talk about another disturbing trend: drive-by downloads. When you think of a drive-by, you probably think of someone shooting from a moving car. A drive-by is never a good thing. So, you can guess that a drive-by download is something you do not want to happen to your computer.

On the consumer blog operated by virus provider McAfee, Robert Siciliano defines drive-by downloads as "The unintentional download of a virus or malicious software (malware) onto your computer or mobile device."[18]

What is scary about this type of harmful software is that, by visiting a site, you could trigger an automatic download of venomous software. You will not have to click to start the download. In fact, you may not even realize the download has started.

Let's say you want to go to YouTube.com, but you mistakenly type in yoube.com or youtub.com. You realize your error because the site is either not at all like YouTube or there's something "off" about it. So you back out of the site. Whew! You dodged a bullet, right? Wrong.

The download probably started as soon as you opened the webpage.

"But what about legitimate websites? I'm safe, right?"

Again, I'm going to have to say you're wrong. Sorry. Drive-by hackers often attach code to existing sites that are vulnerable to such attacks. So, it is possible that a site that you have visited (and trust) in the past could suddenly have malicious code embedded in it.

As you can see, hackers are pretty vigilant about getting their hands on your information. I hope I haven't scared you off because we still have more ground to cover. Up next, offline ways thieves operate.

18. Siciliano,2013

CHAPTER 4

Old-School Ways Thieves Can Steal Your Identity

The preferred method that identity thieves use is the Internet. Most people have computers at home—even crooks. Stealing from millions of unsuspecting people all across the world can easily be accomplished with a few simple keystrokes. As we have read, a crook can unleash a bot or a malicious virus without breaking a sweat. However, I don't want you to let your guard down when you are offline. Some crooks use old school methods to get their hands on your personal information.

An identity thief may use an offline method in conjunction with an online scheme as a way to get as much information about you as possible. The more information a scammer can get on you, the better. This is true whether the scammer is a collector or an end user, but especially if the scammers are the collectors. Here's why. Recall that a collector can sell bits and pieces of information on you. The more information these crooks have, the more money they can command.

The goal of this book is to arm you with knowledge to help prevent identity theft online. However, in this chapter we will look at some of the more popular methods and discuss what steps you can take to protect your information from falling into the wrong hands.

PHONE THIEVES

Have you, or someone you know, ever received a phone call claiming they are from Microsoft technical support? This is a phishing scam. The scammer will claim you have an issue with your computer. They will then try to trick you into giving them remote access so they can fix the problem.

They may sound legit because they refer to you by name, but do not be fooled. You can be sure they got your name and number by some other means. Every few weeks I receive a call from one of these bozos. Most of the time I ignore calls from numbers that I do not recognize. But sometimes I will take the call. Here is a typical conversation:

    Me *(in a bored tone)*: Hello
    Scammer: Hi, Myra?
    Me *(still bored)*: Yes
    Scammer: How are you today?
    Me *(getting more bored by the minute)*: Good

Scammer: Great. This is Greg [or John or Pete or Larry] from Microsoft technical support. I'm calling about your computer. We have detected there is a problem with your computer.

Me: Which computer?

Scammer: Yes, your computer running Windows.

Me: Okay, can you be more specific. I need to know which computer?

Scammer: Yes, yes. We are showing that you have a computer running Windows.

Me *(highly annoyed at this point)*: Dude, I need you to be more SPE- CI- FIC. I have multiple computers. I NEED TO KNOW WHICH ONE YOU ARE TALKING ABOUT! [Yes, at this point I'm screaming.]

Now, "Greg" may realize that I am on to him. He may hang up. If Greg is kind of dense, I may egg him on a bit. When I don't feel like playing silly games, I let them know right away that I'm not falling for their snow job. Or I will tell them that it isn't possible that I have an issue with Windows because I am using a Mac or, better still, I am running Ubuntu/Linux.

What happens if you fall for this phishing scam, though? Like most scams, the damage can be devastating. If the scammer gains your trust, they can trick you into installing malicious software. They may ask for your credit card information to bill you for the scam "service" call.

Microsoft warns consumers that they will never "proactively reach out to you to provide unsolicited PC or technical support. Any communication we have with you must be initiated by you."[19] So unless you have placed the call, no one from Microsoft is going to contact you first. If you receive a call, do yourself a favor—hang up.

---

19. Microsoft

The Microsoft scam is popular, but there are many more floating around. Some of the calls people receive are targeted. For example, I receive a ton of scam calls about business loans. Many calls, however, are robocalls. A robocall is a recorded call placed by an automated dialing system. You usually will not speak with a live person, although some will ask you to "hold for the next available representative" or give you the option of pressing a number to speak with someone.

Fast Fact

Politicians often use robocalls to reach potential voters. These types of calls (although sometimes annoying) are not malicious.

Phishing robocalls, on the other hand, have one goal in mind: to steal your money or your identity. Here are a few of the types of calls you might receive:

- A recorded call congratulating you on winning an all-expense paid trip or cruise. The trip could be to an exotic location, like the Bahamas or a U.S. location like Disney World or Las Vegas. You may think this is your lucky day, but the only lucky person in this scenario is the scammer that talks you into giving out your financial information. The trip is free (of course!), but you might have to pay some kind of small fee or they might need the information for ID verification purposes.

- Offers of free trips or merchandise for taking a survey. This is a variation on the above theme. You still win a free trip or merchandise, but the catch is you need to complete a short survey first. This way it seems like you are not getting something for nothing. You are providing them with data after all. So after asking you a few bogus questions, the trip or merchandise is yours. But first . . . "We need your Social Security number, date of birth, mother's maiden name . . ." Again, you can kiss that trip and your personal data goodbye.

- A message supposedly from your credit card company calling about an issue with your card or offering to lower your interest rate. I have gotten several calls from these scammers. They pretend they are calling from your credit card company, but they never identify themselves other than something along the lines of "Card member services." They will proclaim the good news—that you can lower your interest rate—but first you need to verify a bit of personal information. Not!

- Someone pretending they are calling from the Internal Revenue Service (IRS). This is a tasty little scheme making the rounds. You answer your phone and you hear a terse, recorded message supposedly from the IRS claiming you have a tax issue that must be settled IMMEDIATELY. They often threaten legal action or to send the police to your house if you ignore the message. Maybe you recently started a part-time job after school and last year you filed taxes for the first time. Perhaps you are worried that you did something wrong. If you receive a call like this, do not panic. It is a scam. Like Microsoft, the IRS will never initiate a phone call to you regarding a tax issue.

GRAB AND RUN

With today's high-tech thievery, it seems almost comical that a crook would resort to the old grab and run. But they do. In a grab and run, a crook will do exactly that—grab your purse, book bag, wallet, suitcase—and run. At one time you might run after the crook, but with gun violence being rampant, most people will not risk their lives in hot pursuit.

If you live in a large city or near a tourist hotspot, pickpockets are still common. If someone bumps up against you, there is a good chance they may walk off with your wallet. They will not only have your money, but your bank or credit card and your driver's license. They could potentially walk away with your Social Security card, passport, or other important documents too.

So do these crooks just grab the first purse or wallet they see? Usually not; although some crimes can be crimes of opportunity. For example, if you leave your purse unattended, even for a few seconds. Most thieves look for items that are easy to snatch. For instance, a purse falling off your shoulder or a loosely held one. They may go for a big purse because they figure it has a lot of loot. If you are rocking a Louis Vuitton, Prada, Tory Burch, Fendi, Guicci, or other designer bag, a thief may grab it—not only for what's inside, but because they can make a little extra cash selling the purse.

Guys, if your wallet is peeping above the pocket line, it's like a beacon to sticky fingers. They may not even have to do the old bump and grab — it is possible they can wiggle it out without you feeling a thing.

Crooks check to see if the wallet is sticking above the pocket line, which makes reaching for it much easier. In one feathery light movement, they will relieve you of your wallet. The remedy is to use a wallet small enough to fit completely in your pocket. If possible, do not use a wallet at all.

If you are traveling alone, you are also more at risk. As stated above, most people will not chase after a purse snatcher, especially if they are alone. But it is possible that if you are traveling with one or more person, some may run after the grabber.

Crowded areas are best for these types of crimes. Tourists are usually good targets. Can you guess why? That's correct! Tourists are too busy *oohing* and *ahhing* over the sights to notice what is going on around them. Even if you are not a tourist, you should remain alert when you are away from home.

At this point, you may wonder whether you should leave your purse or wallet at home altogether when you go out. You can, or you can follow these safety tips:

- When selecting a bag, choose one that is not easily accessible to a villain, especially when travelling in a crowed area. For example, do not use a fanny pack or a bag that you wear on your back or sling across your shoulder. A better choice is one that crosses over your chest or securely sits under your arm.

- Carry only as much cash as you will need for one day. Leave credit and bank cards at home unless you absolutely need them.

- Bags with zippers are more secure than those with snaps, fabric fasteners, ties, or other loose types of closures.

- Do not place items in your back pocket. Just like your wallet, a skilled thief can easily relieve you of your possessions by either a bump and grab or, if it is visible, by simply lifting it.

TRASH AND DUMPSTER DIVING

You may have heard of dumpster diving. Typically, frugal individuals sort through dumpsters looking for items they can salvage. As the saying goes, "One man's trash is another man's treasure." Most of these guys are harmless. They are looking for treasures they can recycle.

Realizing that most of us do not take precautions when discarding sensitive information, identity thieves are willing to sort through our trash, hoping to hit the jackpot. Sometimes the crooks simply walk up to your mailbox and take your incoming mail.

You may not think twice about throwing away your cellphone bill. But you should. The rule of thumb is any document that contains account numbers, your name and address, your signature, personal information about your whereabouts, medical information, employment history, or Social Security number should be shredded before you trash it. The types of information they will take include:

- Credit card offers

- Bank statements

- Expired driver's licenses, passports, and IDs

- Medical records and information

- Travel itineraries

- Old bills

SKIMMING

Unlike the previous methods of identity theft, skimming is something that is completely out of your control. I have explained how you can avoid phishing expeditions and encouraged you to shred your sensitive data before putting it in the trash. But skimming is difficult to prevent because you are not engaging in any type of negligent behavior that would cause the loss of your personal information.

First, let me explain what skimming is. You may have heard the term before, maybe in a news story about someone "skimming off the top." A businessman may try to pay less income tax by not reporting all of his cash receipts. This is a form of skimming. Even crooks skim from each other. Suppose a couple of grab-and-run thieves are in cahoots. They agree to divvy up the proceeds from their illegal deeds. Crook A does not want to share *all* the stolen booty with Crook B, so he decides to skim a little off the top before they meet up. He might, for example, take some of the cash or one or two credit cards.

For identity theft purposes, skimming is when someone, who legitimately has a reason to have your bank or credit card, makes a copy of the information for later use. Recall the earlier example of the McDonald's drive through employee who took pictures of customers' cards with her cell phone? This is an example of skimming.

Skimming can happen whenever your card is out of your possession—especially when it is out of your line of vision. Retail stores are big culprits, as are hotels and restaurants. The waiter that walks away with your card to ring up dinner could very well skim your information.

I have already mentioned that an employee can snap a pic with their cell phone. They could also go old school and write down the information: credit card number, expiration date, and security code.

There are also skimming devices that crooks can use to steal your information. The devices are attached to card readers at places like ATMs and gas pumps. When you swipe your card, the skimming device reads your information. Then, it stores the info for later use by these crooks. In cases like this, there is really nothing that can be done, because you will not be aware that your card has been skimmed until someone uses your card.

SMISHING

You are probably asking, "What in the world is 'smishing?" No, it is not a word I made up (although I wish I had), but it refers to phishing done through a Short Message Service (SMS)—or text message, as it's commonly called.

As with all other phishing scams, the text message will arrive, often with some sense of urgency. You may be told, for example, that there is an issue with your bank account or credit card. You may be told to call a number to verify information, otherwise the bank will freeze your account. They may spoof a number to fool you into thinking you are receiving a message from someone you trust. The message will include a link, and if you click on it you will probably download malicious software.

I received a message supposedly because I was tagged in someone's Facebook photo. I was supposed to clink the link to see the image. The problem was, I had no idea who this person was, so there was no way I was going to click that link.

I really hope I have not scared you too much. Now that you understand how serious an issue identity theft is, we will look at some typical scams that should be on your radar.

CHAPTER 5

So far, this guide has highlighted different methods scammers use to try and trick you. I feel confident that the next time you see a phishing email, you will hit the delete button. Let's turn now to scams that look legitimate but are as stinky as a locker room after a football game. It's impossible to list all of the scams currently in circulation — this book would weigh so much, someone would have to help you carry it.

This chapter looks at some of the most common scams you will find online today. Identity thieves spend a lot of time looking for new ways to steal from potential victims. New cons pop up every day. Right now as you read this book, someone is sitting at a computer plotting. The tools and information in this book will help you stay smart about identity theft and avoid becoming a victim, but that is only the first step. You need to stay informed.

Auction Scams

Here's a question for you. When you're looking for a great deal, do you visit auction sites like eBay, eBid, or Overstock.com? If you said yes, you're not alone. About 35 million people have participated in online auctions at some point.[20] Identity thieves follow the money. They know that millions of people visit auction sites. That means millions of identities are up for grabs.

When you visit an auction site and an item catches your eye, you may think there's no harm in bidding. But, you should proceed with caution. Even if the website is legitimate, you cannot always trust the seller.

I am not a crook, but in less than five minutes I created a fake account at a popular auction site. I won't point fingers, but trust me—it's not hard for a scammer to do the same. Don't worry, I deleted the account.

The point is, a dishonest person can easily upload fake pictures of "for sale" items. In this scheme, you will never get your product—but the faker will have your money.

Other scammers will send you an inferior product. Good luck getting a refund. Many items are sold "as is" or there is a no refund policy. Even if

20. Lenhart, 2006

you say the seller misrepresented the product, it could be hard to prove. It becomes a case of "he said, she said." The seller can claim you damaged the product or that it was shipped as described.

These annoyances are nothing compared to what happens if you buy from an identity thief. In the above examples, although the sellers are crooks, they are crooks of a different kind. They want your money, not your identity. Paying for an item you never receive will lighten your wallet, but your identity will remain intact.

Using an auction as a cover to steal identities gives the scammers access to your financial and other personal information. Since these thieves are good at covering their tracks, catching them is nearly impossible. When it comes to online auction scams, thieves have found a surefire way to grab your information. Sometimes they work with another scammer—a fake escrow site.

Fake escrow websites

While some scammers like to work alone, many crimes aren't committed by a leaderless group of thugs. Instead, you are more likely to get duped by a well-organized gang with a leader calling the shots—or at least two fools working together.

You are probably wondering what "escrow" means, so let's get that settled first. Dictionary.com defines escrow as, "A deed, a bond, money, or a piece of property held in trust by a third party to be turned over to the grantee only upon fulfillment of a condition." [21]

---

21. Dictionary.com, 2016

Suppose a classmate received the new PS4 for his birthday. He wants to unload the PS3 that is collecting dust in his room. You (poor thing) are still rocking a PS2, so you jump at the chance to upgrade your system.

But there is a problem. Neither of you seem to trust the other.

> **Seller:** Give me the money and I'll bring the system tomorrow.
> **You:** Um, no. Bring the system, *then* I'll pay you.
> **Seller:** Look, I don't wanna lug this thing all the way to school if you don't have the money.
> **You:** Well, I'm not gonna give you my money. You might "forget" to bring the system.

At this point, you and the seller are at an "impasse"—you are deadlocked and neither of you will budge.

One option is to have an impartial third party act as the escrow holder. You give this trusted person your money, and he or she holds it until you receive the item. When you are satisfied, then the seller receives payment.

Fake escrow sites take advantage of buyers' fear of getting cheated. When your bid is the winning offer, you want to make sure you actually receive the item. Some turn to escrow services. The buyer deposits money into an account held by the service until the buyer receives the product. Once the buyer agrees the product was received as expected, the escrow service is notified to release the funds to the seller.

You can find legitimate escrow services online, but make sure you thoroughly research the company first. You do not want to become a victim twice—from both the seller and the escrow service working together.

ADVANCE FEE (NIGERIAN) SCAMS

You may have heard of advance fee scams — commonly called the Nigerian scam. Allegedly this sting originated in Nigeria. However, an advance fee scammer could live across the globe from you — or across town.

The con takes different forms:

- You may receive a message from a rich person (or member of a royal family) begging for your assistance in getting money out of their country.

- You may receive a congratulatory email claiming you have won MILLIONS of dollars.

- You may receive an "official" email from the FBI or U.S. Treasury claiming you have a suitcase full of money or valuables waiting for you at the airport.

- Sometimes a rich person is dying and out of the blue wants to leave their loot to you.

These scams have one thing in common — they entice victims into paying a fee in order to receive money or valuables. If you fall for the con, not only will you not see a penny, but you might also lose a lot of your own money or your identity.

If you receive one of these phishing messages, you may think it's your lucky day. Just remember, if something sounds too good to be true — it probably is.

More troubling than the loss of money is the loss of your identity. Let's say the sender did not ask for money. Maybe they claim you won a lottery. Once the thief has your attention, the next step is to trick you into handing over your banking and other personal information.

Here's how. Let's go back to my inbox and take a closer look at one of these scams. I received this "official" letter from FBI Agent Mark Giuliano:

> Attention: Beneficiary,
>
> We sincerely apologize for sending you this sensitive information via e-mail instead of certified mail, post-mail, phone or face to face conversation. It's due to the urgency and importance of the security information of our citizens.

Wait a minute. You're concerned about sending me secure information, but you go ahead and send it by email where it could fall into the wrong hands? Please, go on.

> I am Agent Mark Giuliano from the Federal Bureau of Investigation (FBI) Field Intelligence Groups (FIGs). We intercepted two consignment boxes at JFK Airport, New York. The boxes were scanned and they contained large sums of money ($4.1 million),

> also some backup documents that bear your name as the
> Beneficiary / Receiver. An investigation was carried out on the
> diplomat that accompanied the boxes into the United States and
> he stated that he was to deliver the funds to your residence as an
> overdue payment owed to you by a foreign country.

Hold up. I hate to keep interrupting you, but dude, really? First of all, the FIGs acronym reminds me that I need a snack. Second, who walks around with $4.1 million in cash? Ever heard of Traveler's Checks? Wire transfer? Cashier's check? No, this "diplomat" is walking around with *boxes* of cash. Okay, let's keep going.

> After cross-checking all legal documents in the boxes, we found
> out that your consignment was lacking an important document
> and we can't release the boxes to the diplomat until the document
> is found, we have no other option than to confiscate your
> consignment.
>
> According to Internal Revenue Code (IRC) in Title 26 also contain
> reporting requirements on a Form 8300, Report of Cash Payment
> Over $10,000 Received in a Trade or Business, money laundering
> activity may violate 18 USC §1956, 18 USC 1957, 18 USC 1960, and
> provision of Title 31, and 26 USC 6050I of the United States Code
> (USC), this section will discuss only those money laundering and
> currency violations under the jurisdiction of IRS, your consignment
> lacks proof of ownership certificate from the joint team of IRS and
> IRC, you're requested to reply back immediately for direction on
> how to procure the fund ownership certificate to avoid being
> charged for evading the law, which is punishable offense in the
> United States.

At least this crook is trying to make his letter look official by throwing around a bunch of IRS codes.

You are required to reply within 72 hours or you will be prosecuted in a court of law for money laundering, you are instructed to desist from further contact with any bank(s) or person(s) in any part of the world regarding your payment because your consignment has been confiscated by the Federal Bureau of Investigation here in the United States.

Yours In Service,
Agent Mark Giuliano
Regional Deputy Director
Field Intelligence Groups (FIGs)

Whoa, did this dude just accuse me of money laundering?

Question: Since the "agent" did not ask for money, is this still a scam?

Answer: The simple answer is yes. Let me explain. The email requested that I contact him within 72 hours to clear up this matter. Most people will recognize this as a hoax and ignore Agent Mark. However, if you are the nervous type and you want to assure the feds that you are not a money launderer, you will reply so that you can clear your good name. Or maybe you believe there are actually boxes full of money with your name on it. Either way, you fall for the bait. The "agent" assures you the matter can be resolved easily. All you have to do is prove your identity. If you are still on the hook, you will give the "FBI" information that will verify who you are: name, address, date of birth, Social Security number, driver's license number, etc.

By now you can guess you will not see the four millie, but the scammers will drain you of every cent you have. Plus, they will probably open up a few new accounts and drain them.

Here is another (unedited) example. I received this message from "Christy Walton." The real Christy Walton is the widow of John Walton, whose father was Sam Walton of Wal-Mart and Sam's Club.

> My Dearest,
>
> Greetings to you my Dear Beloved,
>
> I am Mrs Christy Walton, a great citizen of United States. I bring to you a proposal worth $5,000,000,000.00 which i intend to use for CHARITY.

Okay, so right out the gate, this chick has a billion-dollar proposal for me—a person she has never met! But let's read on; I'm intrigued.

> I am happy to know you, but God knows you better and he knows why he has directed me to you at this point in time so do not be afraid.

Oh, *now* I understand! God told her, so it's all good.

> i saw your e-mail contact at ministries of commerce and foreign trade departments.

What? Why is my email . . . never mind.

> i am writing this mail to you with heavy sorrow in my heart, It is painful now to let you know that I have been suffering from a Heart disease for the past 22 years and just few weeks ago my Doctor told me that I won't survive the illness.

Please stop randomly capitalizing words that do not need to be capitalized. While you're at it, please start capitalizing words that should be capitalized.

my name is Mrs. Christy Walton a great citizen of United States of America, and am contacting you because i don't have any other option than to tell you as i was touched to open up to you about my project. Please reply me back if you are interested, so i can provide you with further details.

God Bless You.

Please reply me back if you are interested, so i can provide you with further details.

Mrs. Christy Walton
www.forbes.com/profile/christy-walton

Christy, Christy, Christy—*girlllllll,* can you please stop this foolishness? By the way, who goes around saying they are a great citizen of the United States of America? I love how "Christy" attaches a profile piece from *Forbes* on the real Christy Walton. I guess she was trying to prove she is a real person (but we know better).

"Christy" did not ask me for money. This has to be legit, right? Nope. If I contact "Christy," she will come up with a reason to request personal information. She will probably ask for my bank information. How else am I going to get my $5 billion?

Do we have time for one more? Yes, I think we do. I received this "urgent" message just the other day.

Attention: ,

Come on now Mr. or Ms. Spammer, geez you forgot to add a name!

> Hope you're doing good? I have discussed with my boss on the release of your fund and was informed that he spoke with the president of African Development Bank and they both agreed to work together and secure the release of the fund without any hassles. It is also very important that we also play safe to avoid any complication cos the FBI and other similar agencies are bent on tracking large sums of money being transferred to Europe and America due to the rise of insurgence.

So, I guess I'm supposed to know you and your boss? Let me see if I follow:

1. A bank in Africa has my money.

2. The bank, along with "the boss," is conspiring to evade the watchful eye of the FBI so that I can receive the funds they are holding hostage.

(Let's all pretend we didn't see "cos.")

To continue:

> To achieve success, we are going to have this fund split into
> different bank account in few countries and then proceed to
> obtain clearance and fund release order from those banks using
> the influence of the president of African development bank. In
> view of this, will have to visit those countries as at when those
> transfers will be made so that our associates over there will have
> it recorded and verified with immigration that you indeed visited
> the country.

So, you will divide my money into little bundles, then place the packs in a
"few" countries. Plus, you expect me to zoom around the world to retrieve
MY money. I don't fly, so this would not work for me. But continue.

> You also do not need to bother about the cost of travel as we have
> arranged with a financier who will take responsibility for your
> flight tickets, hotels and cash for other expenses that might
> accrue in the cause of your trip. agreement with the financier is
> that he will get 20% of the total sum ($2m usd) once it has been
> remitted to you.
>
> The financier is concerned about your sincerity to abide by this
> agreement and i have given him my word that i trust you will not
> disappoint.
>
> Your first trip will take you to India, Holland , Australia or Italy and
> you will need to apply for visas if need be.

Great, so I don't need to worry about travel costs. All I need to do is pay 20
percent of the $2 million.

> Most importantly, remember that details of this transaction should be kept confidential as you're aware that it is against the thics of our profession to aid a beneficiary or release some vital information's from the bank, and none of us will want to get in trouble with the law.

You are concerned about the confidentiality of this illegal deal, but you send it via email. Okay.

> Please re-confirm your details to avoid any error:
>
> NAMES:
> D.O.B:
> Place of birth:
> Sex:
> Marital status:
> Address:
> Phone numbers:
> Email address:
> Occupation:.........
>
> Confirm the receipt of this mail!
>
> Best regards
> Lawrence Green.
>
> Head, foreign remittance
> African Development Bank.
> Discover something new.

This scammer does not beat around the bush. He expects me to reply to this message, confirming my personal information. I love the "Discover something new" tagline at the end of the message. I guess this is supposed to add legitimacy to the scam. Plus, what is "thics"? Ethics, maybe? I don't know.

Okay, all jokes aside. I had fun pointing out how dumb these letters are, but unfortunately these scams aren't jokes, because many people fall for them every day.

Some scams are easy to spot (like the above examples). Other scammers are a bit more sophisticated. If you are still not sure what to look for, here are some signs:

- You receive an email with a subject line marked URGENT or CON-FIDENTIAL, in all caps. This is a ploy to get your attention.

- You receive a message that is not addressed personally to you. These messages are usually part of a bulk mail out.

- You receive a message that shouts the dollar amount by writing in all caps—TEN MILLION DOLLARS. Just like the subject line, the crooks are trying to get your attention.

- Watch out for relatives of a rich deceased person who claim you have been left money.

- Do not trust messages from barristers, doctors, government officials, or religious figures. They are all scammers.

These con artists will always give you specific instructions on what to do next. They may include the information in the phishing message or trap you later if you respond.

The bottom line: a random person will never contact you and offer you large sums of cash or expensive merchandise. If you receive one of these messages, delete it immediately.

CHARITY SCAMS

Your parents have probably taught you that it is better to give than to receive. You hear a lot about paying it forward, and schools routinely have charity drives. These types of crimes are the worst of the bunch. Charity scammers take advantage of the kindness of others—they prey on people's desire to help those who have been affected by illness, disease, or natural disasters.

I survived Hurricane Katrina in 2005. I vividly remember many charitable people stepping in to offer assistance. I also remember many scams that surfaced. Some people set up fake websites to lure money out of the pockets of people who wanted to help, for example.

Look, I don't know you personally, but I can sense you have a good heart. So, let me warn you against the dangers of falling for charity scams.

Here are some important tips to remember about charity scammers:

- Scammers often buy domain names similar to well-known charities (as we have previously discussed in Chapter 3). For example, Red-Cross.com. They hope that you will not notice that the URL of the real Red Cross is RedCross.org.

- They may spoof a legitimate website, then redirect you to the site from their fake charity page. They are hoping you don't realize you are not on the legitimate site.

- They may send phishing emails with links to the charity's website. Of course, the link redirects you to a fake page.

- They often use offline methods, too. You may get call or letter, usually from someone claiming they are from an organization like a police or fire association. Or they will set up outside a big box store or other heavily-trafficked area. They often claim they're raising money for a church or school organization.

- Sometimes you give to a legitimate charity but still get ripped off. Identity theft is often an inside job. Just because a charity is legitimate, does not mean all of the employees are.

The takeaway is this: do not respond to any phishing emails or calls asking for a charitable donation. If you want to contribute, check the official website of well-known charities. It is a good idea to ignore everyone else. It is possible the charity may be legitimate, but it is better to be safe than sorry. The other sad thing about these types of crimes is legitimate charities often suffer loses. If you have been swindled before, you may think twice about giving again.

It's bad enough to lose money to a charity scam. But if you have given the crooks your credit or bank card information, they can steal your identity as well.

SOCIAL CATFISHING

I admit I had not heard of catfishing until the Manti Te'o story exploded in the news in 2013.

A catfish is a person who "sets up a false personal profile on a social networking site for fraudulent or deceptive purposes." [22]

If you're not familiar with Te'o's fish tale, let me see if I can explain it. Here goes:

Te'o, currently a linebacker for the San Diego chargers, met and subsequently began an online romance with a woman named Lennay Kekua. This was when he played for Notre Dame. With me so far?

22. Merriam-Webster, 2016

Okay, so the lovebirds canoodled online, never actually meeting in person. Tragically, she died on the same day Te'o's grandma passed. Allegedly, Te'o's girlfriend survived a near-fatal car accident but was then diagnosed with leukemia. The latter is what eventually "killed" her.

Te'o was praised for his ability to not only play, but to lead his team to victory on the very same day he lost his love and his grandma.

However, something was fishy about this whole girlfriend situation. In January 2013, Timothy Burke and Jack Dickey revealed on Deadspin.com that story was a hoax.[23]

Not the part about his grandma, the part about Lennay. Not only did she not die, but she didn't exist. Okay, she sort of existed. Confused? Yeah, I was too when I heard about it. Let me explain.

The pictures of Lennay that appeared online belonged to a woman who was very much alive and had never met Te'o. In fact, after Lennay's "death," she was shocked to see her picture used by the media. There were also contradictions of when they "met." Some reports said 2009, others 2011 or 2012.

Deadspin's article put a 2011 Twitter exchange timestamp as the beginning of the "relationship." Eventually, it was discovered that Te'o's "girlfriend" was a fella named Ronaiah Tuiasosopo — one of Te'o's acquaintances.

The biggest question is whether Te'o was in on the hoax. He supposedly talked to Lennay on the phone. How is that possible, since she never existed? Some people think he was an innocent victim. Others believe that, at some point, he realized what was happening, but because his popularity was skyrocketing, he played along.

23. Burke and Dickey, 2013

Catfishing is a form of identity theft, since the perpetrator is pretending to be someone else. But how can a catfish victim become the victim of identity theft? In a word—easily. When it comes to romance, humans are sometimes not able to see what's right in front of their face. Once the catfish gains your trust and confidence, you may not think twice about handing over personal information. After all, you are in a relationship, right?

You may not give your boo your Social Security number, but you may give out your banking information, account passwords, or other sensitive information. Remember, scammers sell different levels of information. If a crook can verify information like your date of birth, mother's maiden name, the name of your first pet, etc., they call sell the data to other collectors or end users.

Here is my advice concerning online romance: do not trust or start a romantic relationship with anyone you meet on the Internet without vetting the person first. By vetting I mean you should verify the person is who they say there are. I would not suggest a face-to-face meeting. But it is okay to arrange a video chat. If they make excuses about not being able to connect, this should raise a red flag.

SWEET ONLINE DEALS

I love a bargain. I am betting you do too. Another scam making the rounds offers luxury items at deep discounts. Do not take the bait. Here is an example I received recently:

Free Nike Products Until They Run Out

The subject line screamed from my inbox. *Free* is one of my favorite words, but I recognized this message for what it was — a phishing expedition. The email contained links to a website where, supposedly, I could grab free Nike gear. What do you think would happen if I clicked on the link?

Bingo—I could download malicious viruses or be redirected to a spoofing or phishing website. Maybe both. At the website, potential victims are enticed to enter personal information. This could include your contact information. A scammer can sell this tiny bit of information for a few dollars. Or you may have to pay shipping and handling or a small processing fee. In this case, you will enter your financial information. Why not, when the payoff is a luxury item? You will not get a free Nike product, but you can bet a snake will slither away with your identity.

Fast Fact

Spam emails often have a "click here to report spam" link. This is another way spammers try to give the recipient a false sense of security. If you click on the link, best-case scenario, you verify to a collector that your email contact information is accurate. Worst-case? You download a virus or become the victim of a drive-by download.

COLLEGE SCHOLARSHIPS AND GRANTS

I have a 16-year-old son. College is just around the corner for him. This means we are currently looking for ways to finance his education. Like a lot of high school students and parents, we turn to the Internet to look for scholarships and grants.

There is a lot of information floating around cyberspace. Scammers can hear the frustration in every mouse click. In response, they have devised ways to steal student identities. One ruse is to pose as a service that offers information on college financing. They may claim to handle all of the dirty work by supplying you with a list of grant and scholarship opportunities.

In another scam, they pretend to be the sponsors of the grant or scholarship. For every legitimate service you find online, there is at least one or two scam sites.

You Could Earn Your Degree Debt Free!

The subject line of this recent email screamed at me. To make the message appear official, the message supposedly came from the "Government Grant Database-Financial Aid." This was one of those lazy scammers who did not have the time (or energy) to spoof a believable email address. The return email was: bungmoyo.com. An official government email will originate from a ".gov" domain.

The email did not offer any detailed information, instead it directed me to a website. Are you still with me? What would happen if I took the bait?

Yes, you guessed it! I would have to enter personal information. Since this is a school-related matter, most students or parents might not hesitate to input a Social Security number. This information is needed to get financial aid, right? Yes and no. When you apply for financial aid using the official Department of Education's website, you will have to supply personal information, including your Social Security number. For all other sites, they should not request it.

Here are some other red flags:

- If you are asked to pay an up-front application fee, it could be a scam. The problem with catching this type of swindler is if you do not receive a scholarship, you probably will shrug and move on. To look legitimate, some websites may publish a list of fake recipients.

- A variation on the above theme also involves applicants paying an application fee. But because the scammers figure they will pull in enough money from the con to make a profit, they will award a small scholarship. Suppose the plan is to award a $1,000 scholarship. If the application fee is $20 and 1,000 applications are received, that's $20,000. After awarding the scholarship, the scammers can still make a nice profit.

- You win a scholarship but receive a check for more than expected. When you contact the service, they tell you to deposit the check and send another check for the difference. The original check will bounce, and you will be left without a scholarship. The sly fox has cashed the check and disappeared. Poof. The bank is not amused, and you (or your parents) will have to pay overdraft fees and may have to cover the check or face legal hassles.

- Some services claim that they will absolutely locate a scholarship for you. They will even guarantee it. If you run across a service like this—run away as fast as you can. No one can offer this type of guarantee. You can expect to pay a fee for the service, but you will get nothing in return. Despite their guarantee. The crooks disappear into the Upside Down with your money and your personal information.

When looking for financial aid, stick with known government agencies, websites, and services you can verify. Stay away from outrageous claims and sites that ask for personal information.

CONTESTS, COMPETITIONS, AND AWARDS

Scammers often use contests to entice young people into giving up sensitive financial information. They create contests a student would want to enter. Writing and art competition are good examples. The perpetrator will either steal your money or your personal information. Let's take a look at how this con works.

Suppose you enter a writing contest. You happily pay the contest fee because you have a shot at winning money *and* seeing your work in print. Okay, not a red flag because many legitimate contests require a fee. If you don't win, that's cool. You understand that not everyone can win.

In this scenario, you gladly cough up $20. Now, add your twenty bucks to all of the other twenty bucks paid by bright-eyed hopefuls. It adds up to big bucks for the scammer. If you don't win, oh well, better luck next time.

Suppose you receive a message that you are a winner. Great! Usually, there's a catch, though. The "winner" usually has to pay for the book containing the winning entries. In this scam, everyone is a winner. The payoff is usually a crappy anthology that no one wants to read.

How can this lead to identity theft? Like all scams, these contests may require applicants to provide personal information. So, take precautions before entering any contest.

EMPLOYMENT SCAMS

For many teens, finding a job is a rite of passage. I got my first job when I was in high school. I worked at McDonald's in a local mall. I knew other teens who worked at fast food establishments, movie theaters, and other entry-level jobs. Today, teens are still grinding away, doing similar work. Some dislike what they are doing but love the paycheck. When a better opportunity comes knocking, an unsuspecting teen might answer the door.

There are a bunch of employment scams making the rounds. Teens are sometimes the target, or they fall into the trap by accident. Either way, these positions do not exist. If you receive a phishing email, delete it. If someone robocalls you about a job, hang up. If you happen upon a website touting jobs for everyone, keep it moving.

What does an employment scam email look like? I told you earlier I receive tons of spam, so you can be sure I received at least one while writing this book (I actually received *way* more than one). Here is what a typical message may look like:

Re: Salary [$1500 /week]

Hello!

We are looking for employees working remotely. My name is Josefa, I am the personnel manager of a large International company. Most of the work you can do from home, that is, at a distance. **Salary is $2300-$5700.** If you are interested in this offer, please visit **Our Site**

Best regards!

There's no beating around the bush in this message. Instead, a simple offer of employment. Can you spot why this is a fake? Here are a few clues:

- The message is a typical message sent in bulk with no personalization. [Hello!]

- A message from an actual business contact would use their full name. [Josefa]

- A business would include the full name of the company. [a large International company]

And what is the deal with that fuzzy math? The header states, "$1500 a week", but in the body of the salary is "2300-$5700." This does not add up. Plus, the salary is unclear. Is it $2300 – $5700 an hour, week, month, year?

The funniest part of this email was the return address. The message was from "Nadja," but she calls herself "Josefa" in the body. Does she not know her own name? I am beginning to sound like a broken record, but if it sounds too good to be true, it probably is.

These scams are excellent ploys to get you to turn over your personal information, particularly your Social Security number. You can be sure that legitimate companies do not send out bulk employment messages looking for workers. If you see an email like this, delete it. The work from home option is particularly interesting to a lot of people, but do not take the bait.

Paid surveys

An offshoot of the employment scam is an offer to earn money taking paid surveys. Like a lot of scams mentioned in this book, you may receive a phishing email or robocall claiming you can make a lot of money by simply giving your opinions via surveys. The email will include a link to a website that will collect your personal information.

Fast Fact

Most paid surveys are either scams or will not pay very much — maybe a few dollars through checks or gift cards. Releasing your personal information hoping for a big payoff is a gamble you do not want to take.

Don't get me wrong; there are companies that pay for your opinion. Over the past year, I have worked periodically with a company that helps businesses gather marketing data. I have been asked to review apps, give my opinion on matters, and perform other tasks. I will not get rich, but I make a little extra coffee and gas money.

The tasks are always fun, and the payout is quick. Payment is through PayPal, so I did not have to give out my banking information. Most importantly, I thoroughly vetted the company before I decided to sign on. There are similar legitimate companies, but most do not work with teens. So, if someone contacts you, it is probably a scam.

SOCIAL MEDIA SCAMS

In addition to catfishing scams, social media scams targeting teens is hugely popular. Facebook, Twitter, Instagram, and other platforms can put you at risk for a scammer or identity thief.

A popular trick is to reply in the comments section of a popular post. Sometimes the message is in response to the topic. Other times, it is way off base. I was reading a post on Facebook recently about a political debate. Everyone was on topic except one poster, who went on about how she had made a gazillion dollars in two days. A link was included, of course.

In addition to money-making opportunities, you may see links to free movie or music downloads, articles, videos, pictures, and memes—anything that would convince a user to click the link.

Virus provider, Norton, highlighted some scary numbers in a 2012 cybercrime report. [24] On the topic of users of social media platforms:

- 4 in 10 have been victims of a cybercrime

- 1 in 6 report someone hacked their social media account and pretended to be them

- 1 in 10 has fallen for a scam or fake link

- 1 in 5 never bother to check a link before sharing with others

- 1 in 6 do not know their privacy setting (is it private or public?)

- 36 percent accept friend requests from people they don't know

24. Norton, 2012

- 3 in 10 have received a message from a "friend" who they suspect wasn't really a friend

As you can see, these types of risky behaviors leave the door wide open for a scammer to walk through. A lot of what happens on social media is because of the relaxed attitudes of people who use these platforms.

There are many more scams around, but this chapter has highlighted some of the popular ones as of this writing. By the time this book is published, more scams will have surfaced. When it comes to guarding your identity, you have to remain proactive. One way to do that is by keeping well-informed of what is happening in the world of identity theft.

CHAPTER 5

How to Protect Yourself from Becoming a Victim

Since you have made it this far, it means you are serious about not becoming a victim of identity theft. This guide has offered many useful tips on how to protect yourself. Upcoming chapters will dig deeper into important issues, such as how to spot when you have been victimized and what to do when you know the offender.

This chapter offers tips on protecting your identity—both online and offline. The tips are arranged by categories for easy reference.

When you finish reading this guide, I hope you will take the information presented and use it to keep your identity safe. But it does not stop there. For many criminals, scamming innocent victims is a full-time job. They invest a lot of time and effort coming up with new ways to separate potential victims from their money or personal information, but you can thwart them in their path by being vigilant about protecting yourself.

With that in mind, the first and most important tip—one that deserves its own category—is this:

1. Stay up-to-date with all the new ways people are trying to scam you, and learn what you can do to stop them.

PASSWORDS AND PINS

2. Some accounts give you the choice to use a PIN along with your password. This gives you an added layer of security. You may also have the choice to select a security question before you can access your accounts. You should take any additional options given to you. The more layers of protection your account has, the harder it is for a thief to crack it.

3. Try to choose passwords that are easy for you to remember so you do not have to write them down. If you have to write them down, make sure you use a system or code that only you can decipher. If you create an electronic document and store it on your computer, password-protect it. I know, yet another password to remember! Be sure you don't label the document with something obvious like "password" or "username."

4. When someone tries to crack your passwords, they usually try obvious choices like your middle name, birthday, or anything that is easily associated with you. Although it is easier to remember these types of passwords, you are making the hacker's job a lot easier too. Instead, use a random name or make up a word. Here are some examples of bad passwords:

- Your screen or real name

- Password

- The last four digits of your phone number

- Your Social Security number

- 12345678

- Your birthday

- Names of immediate family members

- Common (dictionary) words

- Personal information like drivers' license number, address, name of school, etc.

- QWERTY

- Common phrases like *iloveyou* or *letmein*

- Admin or administrator

When creating your password, follow these tips:

- Your password should include upper and lowercase letters, special characters, and numbers — even if it is not required. The more random the password the better.

- Choose a password with a minimum of eight characters — the more the merrier.

- Break up the word you select by adding special characters or numbers in the middle of the word. People often add these measure to the end or beginning of the word: randomword12345@#$. A better option: rA12n3do4mW5o@r#d#.

- Most people use well-known symbols like & or @. That's fine, but also throw in a few lesser-used characters like {, <, or].

- Do not choose passwords that you think are secret — like your pets' name or favorite teacher — unless you are sure you have not discussed it. This includes information relating to hobbies, your favorite color, etc. We live in a time of oversharing, so it's easy for someone to shadow you online. Finding out information on you is easy for crooks.

- Do not use a variation of the same password. If a crook cracks one code, it will be easier to crack open more accounts. If you used:

  fluffyMarshmallows!4529

  for a password, do not use:

  fLufFymarShMallOWs9254! on another site.

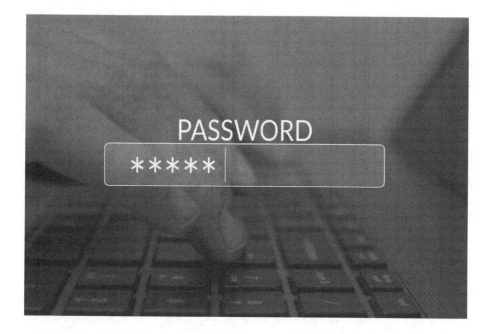

5. Now we come to security questions. When selecting your questions, make sure you choose a question and the answers very, very carefully. If someone can easily guess the answer — then the question wasn't secure in the first place. Choose something obscure, or go ahead and make up an answer. If the question is: What is your favorite color? You could choose the opposite, your least favorite color.

6. If you have the option of selecting the question (some sites will not give you a choice) and you are having trouble coming up with questions, here are some examples you can use:

- Who was my best friend in third (or whatever) grade?

- What is my least favorite subject in school?

- What is my ideal job/career?

- What was the first concert I attended?

- Where did I go for vacation in 2015 (or some other year)?

- What food do I always order at my favorite restaurant?

- How many friends came to my last birthday party?

- What was my favorite Halloween costume?

- Who is my favorite actor?

- Which movie always makes me cry?

7. Make sure you do not save your passwords. I know it is pain to have to sign in to sites you frequent. Anyone with access to your computer can also access any accounts with saved passwords. Clear your browsers cookies (cache) after each use. And uncheck the box that asks if you want to save your password or "remember me."

8. Change your passwords often—at least every four to six months. For some accounts, you will not have a choice. Your password will expire, and you will have to select a new one. Many sites will not let you use a password you have used in the past.

9. Do not give your passwords to family and friends. Not only because they may steal your identity, but they may not be as vigilant about

keeping your information safe. If you absolutely have to give someone your password and or PIN, change it as soon as possible.

10. Get an email account that you can use for activities like confirming registrations for gaming and other sites. I call this my "junk" email account. The email where you receive sensitive information should not be broadcasted. This will help keep your data safer.

PROTECTION FROM HACKING AND SPYWARE

11. Invest in an anti-virus program. The firewall that comes with your computer can stop some attacks, but for full protection you will need an anti-virus program. Symantec's Norton Security and McAfee are good options. Most software will automatically check for and download updates. New threats evolve daily. Good programs constantly update their software to stay ahead of the hackers and make sure you are protected.

12. Be vigilant when downloading anything from the Internet from some-one you met online. If they want to share a picture, suggest they up-load it to a free online site, like Flickr. The file could contain spyware (even if the sender is not aware). Peer to Peer (P2P) file sharing web-sites are particularly dangerous and should be avoided. I realize you may want to get the new song, game, or whatever, but anyone can load a maliciously-coded file and offer it as a download to unsuspect-ing users.

13. When sending sensitive data, like making an online purchase, make sure the website you are using is secure. This goes for email and online forms containing sensitive information. A secure site is encrypted. En-cryption scrambles your information. If the information is intercepted, it cannot be read. Only the intended receiver can read the message. You can tell if a site is using the official encryption — Secure Socket Layer or SSL — by checking for the little lock in your browser.

14. If you have to use a wireless network when you are away from home, make sure the network is secure. How can you tell? You should need a password or PIN to log onto the network. Even then, avoid visiting websites where you need to enter personal information.

AVOIDING ONLINE SCAMS

15. If you post your email address online, one way to stop bots from grab-bing it is to write it like this: yourname-at-gmail-com.

16. Once your name appears on a mailing list, you can expect to get a lot of mail. A lot of times when you sign up for something "free," your contact information is sold to marketing firms. Selling data (just your name, address, and email address) is a lucrative business, even for peo-ple who are not trying to scam you. Here are some ways to opt-out:

- Contact each of the big three credit reporting bureaus to opt out of pre-screened credit card offers.

- You can opt-out by calling 1-888-5-OPT-OUT (1-888-567-8688) or going to www.optoutprescreen.com. This is also for pre-screened offers. You can choose to opt-out for five years or permanently.

- Get your name on the Do Not Call list. This should cut back on some of the phishing calls. Sadly, many scammers violate the list and still call. To get your name on the list, go to **www.donotcall.gov**, or call 1-888-382-1222.

- You can also opt-out (five years only) of direct mail solicitations by contacting the Direct Marketing Association:

  DMAchoice
  Direct Marketing Association
  P.O. Box 643
  Carmel, NY 10512
  www.dmachoice.org

USING YOUR COMPUTER

17. When you are working on your computer in a public place, before you enter any passwords or PINs, make sure no one is close enough to see you type in the information (shoulder surfing).

18. If you have to use a public computer to sign into a sensitive account, make sure you clear the cache before you log off. You should also consider changing your password or PIN when you get home.

19. Computers die. When it is time to bury one, do not simply put it out with the trash. Even if the computer will not reboot, the hard drive can be removed. And that's where the good stuff lives. You will need to

thoroughly wipe your drive clean. Enlist a professional to help, or research online and do it yourself.

20. Do not send sensitive data by email. Even if your account is not hacked, the message can be intercepted on the receiving end.

21. Do you use a password after your computer boots up? You should. A hacker can probably eventually figure out your password, but at least it will give you a little time if sticky fingers walk away with your laptop. This short delay could be all the time you need to change passwords and PINs. Plus, it may give you enough time to contact your financial institutions to alert them of a potential threat.

22. When you are in public and you need to step away from your computer, always log off. It does not matter how long you expect to be away. It only takes a few minutes for a friend or co-worker to poke around while you are away.

OFFLINE PROTECTION

23. As mentioned earlier, thieves often walk up to your mailbox and take your incoming delivery before you or a family member has a chance to retrieve it. A mailbox that locks is a better option. Your family should keep an eye on the amount of mail received and not any unusual changes. If your family receives a lot of mail, then suddenly you start receiving less, this is a cause for concern. Watch your mail carefully and contact the post office if you have further concerns.

24. Always keep your Social Security card in a safe place at home. Unless you need your card for a specific reason, it should never leave your house. If you have to take it for verification purposes, return it immediately to the safe spot when you return home.

25. If you have any forms of identification displaying your Social Security number, talk with someone in charge to find out if it is necessary. If not, request to have your information removed. This includes your driver's license, employee ID card, student ID, health insurance card, etc.

26. Sometimes you need money from an ATM, but you are not close to your bank. What are your options? Most of us turn to a privately-owned ATM. I admit, I have used one a time or two. This is not a good idea. They are more likely to have skimming devices attached. If you have to get money, a better option is to find a store that offers cash back (most do) when you make a purchase. Buy yourself a pack of gum, get the money you need, and enjoy the rest of your day.

27. Before using any ATM, there are a few things you want to do. Check for signs of tampering or skimming devices. When entering your PIN, try to obstruct the view of the camera. If a thief has hacked into the system, you can block the information from being read. But do not do anything odd or suspicious because if a guard is watching, he may think you are up to something illegal.

We are almost at the end of our journey. Stay with me a little while longer. The next chapter will walk you through the steps to take if what you have feared most happens—your identity is stolen.

CHAPTER 7

My Identity Was Stolen! Now What?

Despite your best efforts it is possible that a thief could steal your identity. Remember that some cons are inside jobs, so the person stealing could be someone you trust. A skimming device placed on an ATM or at the gas pump will grab your information and you won't know it until it is too late.

If you become a victim, the first thing to do is take a deep, cleansing breathe. Relax. Repairing damage caused by identity theft takes months — years even. You need to have a plan, then work through it. Eventually, you will get your life back on track. Just follow the advice in this guide.

Let's start by identifying common warning signs of identity theft.

IDENTITY THEFT RED FLAGS

Depending on how your information is used, you may not know your identity has been stolen for a long time. As mentioned, most adults are sticklers for checking their reports each year. Parents usually never think to check to see if their child has an open file.

Now that you know the importance of checking your file, I am sure you have or will do so shortly. Should you breathe a sigh of relief if you do not have a file? Yes and no. Yes, because it means your identity is safe (or no one has used it yet). No, because you cannot let your guard down and assume it will not eventually happen. I am not trying to scare you, only make you aware.

What should you look for? Here are some major warning signs.

- You stop receiving bills or account statements. Many people are living the green life by cutting down on the amount of paper they receive. This includes paperless billing or electronic account statements. If you did not sign up for paperless options, but you have stopped receiving bills or statements, this could be a sign of fraud. A scammer may have forwarded your mail to them. If you do not get a bill or statement, you will not notice the mistakes right away. If this happens to you, sign in to your account, then check the mailing address. If it has been changed, contact customer service immediately.

- You receive a call or mail from a collection agency about an account you do not have. If you get a voicemail, especially one that does not ask for you by name, do not figure it's a mistake. Have a parent return the call to find out what is going on. Sometimes it is a simple mistake. My son received several voicemails on his cellphone from a collection agency. However, they did not ask for him by name. When I found out about it, I returned the call. Apparently the call was for a woman who previously had his cell number. The point is, never ignore the calls. It could be a mistake or it could be identity theft.

- You apply for your first credit card, but your application is rejected. Or maybe you apply for credit to purchase your first car, but you are denied. Since you have never had a credit account, your history should be spotless. This is a definite red flag. The lender should tell you in writing why your application was denied. You can use this letter to request a free credit report—even if you have already gotten your free annual report (more on credit reports shortly).

- You try to use your credit or debit card but it is rejected, although you know your balance is enough to cover the purchase. Did you miscalculate or has someone used your card? You need to investigate.

- You notice your garbage has been tampered with. Remember, thieves have absolutely no problems getting down and dirty by sifting through your trash. Unless you see signs of wild raccoons, it is possible someone is trying to get their hands on your information.

- You start receiving a lot of junk mail from companies that clearly provide goods and services to adults. A business will not invest a lot of time and effort attempting to woo an unemployed teen.

UNDERSTANDING YOUR CREDIT REPORT

The best way to make sure no one has stolen your identity is to check your credit report each year. Consumers can order one free annual report from the big three credit reporting bureaus: Experian, TransUnion, and Equifax. If you need to order another copy within the 12-month period, you may have to pay a fee.

You can order a report individually from each of the bureaus or get a copy from all three at www.annualcreditreport.com. It is a good idea to get a copy from each one. You may assume if you find an error on one, all three will have the same error. Not necessarily so.

Fast Fact

Get a copy of all three of your credit reports. One error-free report may give you the impression that everything is OK, but it is possible that the other two have signs of identity theft.

After you receive your credit report, it may look like a bunch of gibberish. Relax, the following information will help you understand how to read it.

YOUR CREDIT REPORT IN A NUTSHELL

Credit reports are organized into four sections. Let's take a look at each one.

Personal Information: This section contains identifying information: your name, Social Security number, date of birth, phone number, employment history, etc. As a minor, unless you have opened a credit account, you should not have a file. If you have a file, your identity has probably been stolen.

The information in this section may have clues that will help figure out who the culprit is. This information is also useful in helping to prove you have been victimized. For example, if a different date of birth is listed, you can present your birth certificate as proof. Using employment history may help you track down who the thief is. Maybe a company where they worked required a photo ID, for instance.

Once you establish your own credit file, make sure you check this section carefully. You may notice some minor variations, but most should not cause concern. For example, your name may be listed as Jane Doe or Jane T. Doe. As long as your middle name starts with a "T," the report is probably accurate. A lot depends on how the business lists you.

I always sign my full name—Myra Faye Turner. Most of my accounts have me listed this way. There are variations: Myra Turner or Myra F. Turner. That's not a problem.

A red flag: Myra J. Turner, Myra Ann Turner or Myra Faye Smith. A situation like this would definitely cause me to contact the credit bureau. Other causes for concern: an incorrect Social Security number linked to your name, incorrect date of birth, or incorrect present or former addresses.

Public Records: This section lists any legal problems attributed to your Social Security number. This includes bankruptcies, foreclosures, tax liens, and other judgments. Since you are just a kid, this section should be blank. If not, your identity was probably stolen *and* the thief has legal issues.

Your credit report does not show routine arrests, but it will show civil judgments against you. This section only includes financially-related crimes. If a crook ran up an $800 cellphone bill in your name and was sued by the carrier, that information would be listed in this section.

Accounts: This section contains your credit history. It lists all of the accounts that have been opened under your name and Social Security number. Each account shows:

- The date the account was opened

- The names associated with the account

- The amount of the loan or credit limit

- Current balance

- Monthly payment amount, if applicable

- Type of loan: it could be an **installment**, meaning you will pay it off at a particular point, or a **revolving line of credit**, like a credit card or merchant (J.C. Penney, Sears) account

- Account status: open, negative, or closed

- Payment history

If your identity has been stolen, this section will give you a full picture of how much damage has been done. It will also help pinpoint when the theft happened.

Credit Inquiries: This section lists requests by others to see your credit report. This is a definite red flag, unless you authorized the inquiry (for example, if you applied for a job that requires a credit check). However, if you see a ton of inquiries, it is possible that someone has swiped your identity.

What will the inquiry reveal? You can find out the name of the business, the date of the probe, and the reason for the request. So if you see an inquiry from Ford Motor Financing, someone attempted to or succeeded in buying a car in your name.

You may see inquiries from pre-approved credit card companies. Again, this should be a red flag, because these guys will not pursue an unemployed teen.

Fast Fact

There are two types of inquiries: hard and soft. Basically, a hard inquiry is one you make when applying for credit or a job. A soft inquiry is made without your knowledge, as in the pre-approved credit card game.

Cracking the credit code

On your credit report, you will notice a bunch of different codes. For example, in the payment history section, you may see a "c" listed on one account. This usually is the code for "collections."

The big three have their own codes. You can find an explanation on your report. However, here are a few of the universal codes you may see:

- **I:** This is an individual account; you are the sole responsible party for the account.

- **J:** This indicates a joint account; both individuals are equally responsible for the account.

- **A:** This means you are an authorized user, but you are not responsible for making payments. For instance, your parents may authorize you to use their credit card.

- **U:** The account is undesignated (not specified).

- **M:** You were the maker of the account and are responsible for payment.

- **T:** The account has been terminated (has ended).

- **C:** You are the co-signer or the co-maker of the account. You will be responsible for payment if the signer or maker defaults.

- **S:** The account is shared but there is not enough information to list it as I or J.

You will also see information relating to the status of the account. This includes the type of account and how well payments are made on the account. Here are some typical codes:

- **O:** The account is currently open.

- **R:** The account is revolving. This means the account is not a loan that has a specific end date. It is a line of credit that you pay over time (like a credit card).

- **I:** The account is paid in fixed monthly installments, like a loan or mortgage payment.

- **1:** Payments have been or are being made as agreed.

- **2:** You are 30–59 days passed the due date.

- **3:** You are 60–89 days passed the due date.

- **4:** You are 90–119 days passed the due date.

- **5:** You are 120 or more days passed the due date.

- **7:** Payments are being made through wage attachments, meaning the payment are automatically sent to the debtor directly from your employer.

- **9:** The account has been charged off as a bad debt.

- **9B:** The debt is in collections.

Contact information for the credit reporting bureaus

The first step in checking whether your identity has been stolen is to get your credit report from the big three reporting agencies. You can get a report by visiting each agency's website or by visiting annualcreditreport.com or calling 1-877-322-8228. Each agency has a fraud department. The contact information is:

Equifax
Fraud Victim Assistance Department
Consumer Fraud Division P.O. Box 740256
Atlanta, GA 30374
Phone: 800-525-6285

Experian
National Consumer Assistance
P.O. Box 9554
Allen, TX 75013
Phone: 888-397-374

TransUnion
Fraud Victim Assistance Department
P.O. Box 2000
Chester, PA 19016
Phone: 800-680-7289

WHO ELSE SHOULD I CONTACT?

Once you know for certain that your identity has been lifted, you need to take certain steps. An identity theft victim may go into shock and not know what to do or who to contact. Luckily, you have this guide. If your identity has been stolen, it is not the time to go into panic mode. You need to get the ball rolling and hopefully stop the crook from doing more damage.

File a police report

Do not let anyone try to convince you that identity theft is a victimless crime. The first person you should call if you have been victimized is the police. You need to file an official identity theft report. Although they may not be able to help you clear many of your issues, the most important thing you can do is document that you are a victim. This important step will also help corroborate your claim when you contact creditors. If you do not have a police report, many creditors will not believe your identity was stolen. Since filing a false police report is a crime, creditors will usually believe you if you take this important step.

If the theft took place in different cities, you should also contact the police in those locations. Finally, make sure you get a copy of each report you filed.

Contacting creditors

With copies of your police reports in hand, the next step is to contact all of the creditors listed on your credit report. Although identity theft is horrible for the victims, the creditors are victims too.

Fast Fact

If a crook took out a loan in your name, the loan company will probably not recover the money — unless the thief is caught and ordered to pay restitution. As pointed out, these crooks are slippery little worms, so in most cases this will not happen.

You will need to prove that you have been victimized. This is where the police report comes in handy. You may also have to file a dispute claim with the creditor.

Contact the Federal Trade Commission

It may seem scary contacting the government, but if you are a victim, the Federal Trade Commission (FTC) is a valuable resource. The FTC has put together a comprehensive website to help identity theft victims. You can access it at www.identitytheft.gov. The site allows you to file a report online and create a recovery plan.

Filing a report with the FTC proves to creditors that you are a victim and not simply trying to get out of paying a debt. In *The Complete Idiot's Guide to Recovering from Identity Theft*, Mari Frank advises victims to create a paper trail of documentation. If you don't, debtors "will assume that the claims of identity theft are fictitious."[25]

25. Frank, 2010

If you are stuck trying to figure out how to compose a letter to send to creditors, sample form letters are included. All you have to do is plug in the details of your case. Be sure to create an account and fill in as much information as possible. Based on your input, your identity theft report and recovery plan is generated from the information you provide. This information can also be used to generate form letters, as mentioned above. If you do not create an account, your information is not saved when you leave the page. You will need to print the report and the recovery plan.

Fast Fact

The FTC does not handle individual complaints, but filing a complaint with the agency is useful in many ways:

- If you have filed a police report, the FTC will coordinate with the local authorities handling your case. They can share valuable information that can help your case.

- The FTC can help investigate the policies that put your identity at risk in the first place. The FTC can investigate a merchant's careless policies and force changes so that other people do not have the same experiences.

OTHER IMPORTANT STEPS TO TAKE

Whew! Dealing with identity theft is a lot of work, but please do not get discouraged. You may not be able to clear all of your issues up in a few weeks, months, or even years, but eventually things will get back to normal. You have contacted the major players, but there's still a few issues you need to address.

Close compromised accounts

If someone has accessed an account that is actually yours, you need to close it immediately. If a new account was opened, the creditor should have closed it when you reported the theft. You need to make sure they followed through or else the crook can continue to cause damage.

Once all of the issues have been resolved, request written confirmation. You do not want a creditor to tell you over the phone that everything is okay (they believe your story, for example), then turn around and report the debt to a collection agency. Keep all of your documentation in a safe place. You never know if a problem will creep up in the future.

Fast Fact

Without proper documentation, it's your word against the accuser's. You definitely do not want any delinquent accounts to impact your future ability to get credit.

Requesting a new Social Security card

The Social Security Administration (SSA) normally issues one Social Security card in your lifetime. If your identity has been severely abused, you can request a new number. The SSA reports: "If you've done all you can to fix the problems resulting from misuse of your Social Security number, and someone is still using your number, we may assign you a new number."[26]

---

26. Social Security Administration Publication, 2016

If you decide to apply for a new number, you will have to:

- Prove your identity

- Provide proof of your age

- Verify that you are a U.S. citizen or show immigration status

- Show evidence the theft is causing you to have serious ongoing issues

You can visit your local office in person or contact the SSA online at socialsecurity.gov. To find your local office, or to get help with any issues, call 1-800-772-1213.

When you discover your identity has been stolen, you need to take immediate steps to prove you are a victim. It is a long process, but if you follow the steps outlined in this guide, you can regain control of your identity.

You will have to prove that you are innocent. Filing reports with your local police department and with the FTC are important steps to take on your road to recovery. It is a lot of work, but you do not have to go alone. Help is available—so take a deep breath and relax.

CHAPTER 3

When the Thief is a Family Member

So far, this guide has focused mainly on identity thieves who are unknown to the victim. Let's turn to a disturbing trend—familial identity theft.

Familial theft happens when the person stealing your identity is a family member. It happens more often than you think. In a report by Javelin Research & Strategy, it was estimated that students are "four times more likely to be victims of 'familiar' fraud, versus all other consumers."[27]

Familiar fraud is twice as devastating for the victim. Identity theft leaves your finances in shambles. But, eventually you repair the damage. When a family member steals from you, the damage to the relationship may not be as easy to mend. The ripples throughout your family can cause additional problems. Family members may take sides, causing further loss.

For our purposes, "family" includes close family friends. When I was growing up, we had "play cousins." A play cousin was not a blood relative, but someone so close to your family that you treated them like an extended member.

---

27. Javelin, 2015

The point is, familiar fraud includes both your blood relatives *and* close friends. These are people you trust and are supposed to feel safe around. We have a tendency to let our guard down around our family. This is why familiar fraud is so easy to commit.

WHO COMMITS FAMILIAR FRAUD

Question: Which family member is more likely to steal your identity?

Answer: As with most cases of identity theft, it is impossible to single out any one particular person more likely to commit this type of fraud.

Fast Fact

Anyone with access to your personal information could potentially become a thief. When it comes to child identity theft, sometimes accessibility and desperation is the driving force behind these crimes.

The caregiver as thief

Parents of young children are often the offender in this type of crime. Not necessarily because they *want* to, but because they feel they have no other choice when faced with a desperate financial situation.

This guide has already stressed that kids are easy targets because they have no reason to check their credit report. A parent with shaky credit may open an account in a young child's name. Maybe they had issues in the past that they have been unable to iron out. A parent may use their child's identity, vowing to pay on time. They aren't trying to cause later hardships for little Johnny. The problem is, most people that have had credit issues in the past, will have similar issues in the future.

Have you ever watched one of the court TV programs? The judge is always astonished when a plaintiff is in court suing a defendant for skipping out on a debt. The plaintiff has usually gotten credit for the defendant because he or she could not because of ugly credit. They seem surprised when the bum does not pay, leaving them holding the bag.

Even with good intentions, stuff happens. When your identity is not on the line, it's easy to walk away from a debt. For some parents (or family members), if this means a black mark on the child's record—oh well.

The crook could be the non-custodial parent that does the filching. Divorces sometimes turn ugly and kids get caught in the crossfire. Or a relative with easy access to your personal information, like a grandmother or aunt, may lift your identity. Most parents simply do not think a relative would commit this type of crime.

Let's look at an example. Suppose a parent is filling out a document—let's pretend it is a school registration form. Just as she finishes penciling in the Social Security number, the doorbell rings. It's "Aunt Susan." Mom invites

"Aunt Susan" inside. Like a good host, she asks if Susan wants something to eat or drink. "I would love some coffee," she replies.

Mom heads off to the kitchen. She does not bother to put the paperwork up. After all, Susan is family. Mom should think twice, though. Susan has never given the mom any hint that she may have sticky fingers. But you can never be too sure. Mom should remove the paperwork when she leaves the room.

For very young children, a fraudster could use their identity for many years before getting caught. If ever. In many cases, the thief feels the crime is justified. Especially if it benefits the child. Here are two scenarios where a family member may use your identity and think they did nothing wrong:

- A parent wants to give her five-year-old child a good start in life by sending him to a private school. But she cannot afford the tuition, there is no payment plan, and she cannot get a loan in her name. She takes out a loan in her young son's name. Her rationale is a good education will benefit her son. Plus, she is going to repay the loan. When her son is an adult, his record will be spotless once again.

- When he was born, family members put money into a college account for a child. By the time the child is a teen, the mother has developed a gambling habit. Since she is an authorized user on the account, she "borrows" money, a little bit at time. Twenty dollars here, $30 there. She promises herself she will replace the money as soon as she scores big. You can probably see where I am headed. She never scores big, and soon the account is thin as a sheet of paper. But, she still continues to think she will be able to replace the money before her son needs it in a few years.

The problem with these and other desperate acts is that, even with good intentions, outside influences can cause things to get twisted. A parent with intentions to repay a loan taken out in their child's name may lose their job and be unable to repay the loan as planned. A gambler never makes that big score. The money is gone; the child's credit is ruined. Now what?

Other family members as the culprit

It is not only immediate family members that have sticky fingers. Familiar thieves include extended relatives, like cousins. It could include people related by marriage. For example, you may feel confident your sister will not steal your identity, but what about her husband? Can you trust your brother-in-law's brother when he comes over for Thanksgiving dinner? What about the play cousin visiting during Christmas break?

Fast Fact

Best friends, neighbors, babysitters — any person visiting your house with access to your personal information could potentially steal your identity.

A good rule to follow: Use the same safety precautions in your home as you would in public. Should you log off your computer when your brother's girlfriend is visiting and you need to step away a minute? Absolutely.

FIGURING OUT WHICH FAMILY MEMBER IS THE THIEF

Your identity has been stolen and you think a family member is the guilty party. You may feel reluctant to confront this person; but remember, identity theft is a crime and you are the victim.

The first step is to figure out who had access to your information. Think back to all of the people who fit in this category. If the theft has been going on for a long time, it may be harder to pinpoint who stole your identity. This is particularly true if the crime was committed years ago but has only recently been detected.

Wouldn't it be nice if the thief suddenly felt guilty and confessed? Chances are, that will not happen. A parent may come clean, but probably no one else will. So, you will have to put on your detective's hat and conduct your own investigation.

One way to check the identity of the thief is to review purchases made in your name. They may provide clues to who the bandit is. If you have suspicions but no proof, you do not want to confront this person, causing more family drama.

Like all cases of identity theft, the best thing you can do is turn the matter over to the police.

WHERE TO TURN FOR HELP WITH FAMILIAR FRAUD ISSUES

Identity theft is a crime. If you learn the thief is a family member, you have a tough decision to make. The most pressing question: Should you call the police?

Your gut instincts may tell you to not get the police involved. Tell your gut to shut up. I understand you may not want to get your family, neighbors, or close friends in trouble. But what is the alternative? You have to consider the big picture. It is your life they are messing with.

If you have any hopes of clearing up any damage to your credit (or legal issues), you have to contact the police. A crime has been committed. You need to document it if you expect to work with creditors to clear your name. If you are not sure, but you have suspicions, the police can start a formal investigation. After you contact the police, follow the same steps previously outlined. It may be hard, but you have to do it. Reporting that a crime has been committed against you is the only chance you have of restoring your credit.

CHAPTER 9

Identity Theft Protection: What's Available?

Our journey is almost over. But before I let you go, we have a few more areas to cover. Although the future of identity theft may look grim, there is hope.

Thieves are working harder every day to use technology to commit these heinous crimes. They are smart, but you are smarter. You get an A+ for completing this guide. You are well on your way to protecting your identity. In addition to the steps outlined in this guide, you can take further precautions to safeguard your identity. What else can you do?

The information you have read may have left you feeling paranoid or afraid. Do not worry, help is available. In this chapter, you will learn about some of these resources.

CAN A COMPANY REALLY PROTECT MY IDENTITY?

If a company claims to protect you from identity theft, be wary. As you have read, no one is immune from identity theft. A business claiming otherwise is fibbing. So what can these companies do? They can monitor your identity or credit. They can then alert you when suspicious activities appear on their radar. Most offer identity theft insurance, which will help you recoup some of the costs if you are a victim.

Let's look at the difference between the types of monitoring and fraud alerts.

Identity theft monitoring: If you sign up for identity theft monitoring, the company will receive an alert when an activity signals possible identity theft. Red flags could include a request for a change of address and arrest or court records.

Credit theft monitoring: This service monitors one or more of the big three reporting agencies and reports any suspicious activity. This might include changes to your personal information or when a new credit account is opened. These are obvious red flags. Less suspicious activity could go unnoticed until it is too late. If a business checks your credit history, this could signal that someone is using your Social Security number to look for work.

Recovery Services: If your identity is stolen, a recovery service will hold your hand as you navigate the process of cleaning up the damages. They may, for example, assist you in writing letters to the creditors.

Identity Theft Insurance: Humans get insurance to protect the things they love—cars, homes, people. So why not get identity theft insurance? That is a good question. A plan typically covers any of your out-of-pocket expenses related to recovering from identity theft. Is this a good option? Keep in mind, this insurance will not reimburse you for the money you lost. There is usually a deductible—an amount you will have to absorb before the company pays you anything. So, if you have a $300 deductible and your out-of-pocket expenses is $400, the insurance would only reimburse you $100.

Should you invest money in these types of services? This is a personal decision. You will have to weigh the pros and cons to decide. There are free resources available to you, so keep that in mind before you decide to go with a paid plan. A good resource to use is identitytheft.gov.

If you decide that a paid service is what you want, thoroughly vet the company first. Find out exactly what services they offer. Look for complaints (check the Better Business Bureau) online. You want to make sure the company is legit. Remember, identity theft is often an inside job, so it is possible that the company you trust to monitor your identity is a fake one set up to steal your information.

To get you started, here is a list of three top-ranked companies, based on customer reviews:[28]

---

28. Bestcompany.com, 2016

LifeLock
60 East Rio Salado Parkway
Suite 400
Tempe, AZ 85281
1-800-543-3562
www.lifelock.com

LegalShield ID Shield
One Pre-Paid Way
Ada, Oklahoma 74820
(580) 436-1234
www.LegalShield.com

IdentityForce
40 Speen Street
Suite 403
Framingham, MA 01701
1-877-694-3367
www.identityforce.com

CREDIT REPORT FREEZING

Also known as a security freeze, credit report freezing limits access to your report from third parties. So, if someone tries to open a new credit account, the lender will not be able to access your credit report unless you are contacted first.

You will need to contact each of the big three to request a freeze on your report. A small fee is usually charged to freeze and unfreeze your report. The amount of the fee is based on your home state. The cost is usually free for victims of theft and certain age groups. People under 16 and over 62, for instance, usually will not have to pay the fee.

If you need to unfreeze your report, it may take a few days. So plan accordingly. If you apply for a job that you know will require a credit check, you will need to unfreeze your report well before your interview. You will want to unfreeze your account whenever you apply for credit. Again, you have to plan in advance. You cannot decide on the spur of the moment that you are tired of riding the bus, subway, or bumming rides from friends and decide to get your own wheels. If you need financing, you will have to lift the freeze in advance.

If you have been a victim of theft, you definitely want to place a fraud alert on your file. An alert sends a red flag to any lender accessing your file in response to a credit or employment application.

Fast Fact

You can place a fraud alert for free by contacting each of the big three credit reporting bureaus: Experian, TransUnion, and Equifax.

Websites for additional information

This guide is only the first step in making sure you understand identity theft. The changing face of this crime makes it almost impossible to keep up-to-date on what is happening in the world of cybercrime. The best place to turn for current information is the Internet. Here are some of the best websites for identity theft information:

The Federal Trade Commission's site on identity theft
www.identitytheft.org

Privacy Rights Clearinghouse
www.privacyrights.org

The Internet Crime Complaint Center
www.ic3.gov

Fight Identity Theft
www.fightidentitytheft.com

National Organization for Victims Assistance
www.trynova.org

CONCLUSION

Identity theft is a serious crime affecting the young and the old. Not even celebrities or the dead can escape the grip of identity thieves. Although having your identity stolen is a scary situation, this guide has shown you that over time, you can recover.

I applaud you for taking the first step in learning about this serious crime. You picked up this book and you read it from cover to cover. The roadmap presented you with information that will help you identify scammers. It has given you the tools you need to stop phishing expeditions. When you use social media platforms, you will not be so quick to share personal information.

You also realize that the ones closest to you are sometimes the ones who hurt you. The good news is that you will recover. Now that you are armed with the tools you need to protect your identity, do not put this book down and never think about your safety again. Use the information contained in this guide, but don't forget to stay up-to-date on new scams.

Spread the word about identity theft! Stay safe.

Adware: Software that is supported by advertising. Many users agree to adware to get free software. Malicious adware is often bundled with software and downloaded without the approval of the user.

ARPAnet: An early computer networking system used by government agencies to communicate with each other. The ARPAnet evolved into today's Internet.

Backdoor: A way to bypass a computer's normal authentication process, usually for illegal purposes. Also called a trapdoor.

Black hat hacker: An expert computer specialist who uses his skills to scam, spread viruses, or otherwise wreak havoc on a computer or computer network.

Blue hat hacker: An outside computer security expert, hired by a company prior to the launch of a program. Their job is to look for system vulnerabilities.

Cache: Data stored on a user's computer so the same information can be easily retrieved later.

CAPTCHA verification: A test websites use to make sure the user is human and not a computer robot.

Cookies: Small files stored on a user's computer. Cookies can enhance a user's online experience by sending pages tailored to the user's likes. They can also be used to spread viruses and to unknowingly track a user's online movement.

Deadlock: A situation where two opposing sides are unable to come to an agreement.

Distributed Denial-of-Service (DDoS) attacks: An assault on a website, making it impossible for users to gain access.

Dupe: To fool or deceive.

End user: A person who eventually uses a product.

Escrow: Money or property held by a third party until the terms of an agreement have been fulfilled.

Fullz package: A full package of information on an individual, sold to identity thieves.

Grantee: The recipient of a transfer of property.

Gray hat hacker: A computer expert who straddles the lines between being a good (white hat) and bad (black hat) hacker. They may hack into a system to expose vulnerabilities but usually will not cause any malicious damage.

Hacker: A person who breaks into a computer system or network.

Hoodwink: To trick or con.

Identity theft: Illegally obtaining and using another person's information, usually for financial gain.

Impartial: To treat everyone fair; not biased.

Impasse: Unable to reach an agreement.

Inferior: Something of poor quality.

Internationalized Domain Name (IDN): An Internet domain name that can include non-English characters and letters. Arabic, Latin or Chinese script, for example.

Internet Protocol (IP) address: An assigned sequence of numbers that shows the location of a computer on a network.

Keylogging: Illegally recording the keystrokes on a computer, usual done from a remote location.

Keystroke: The tap of a key on a computer keyboard.

Ledger: A book that shows the amount of money received and paid out.

Legitimate: According to the law; legal.

Malware: Malicious software used to spread viruses or cause damage to a computer or network.

Perpetrate: To commit a crime or do something illegal.

Phishing: A scam aimed at tricking someone into giving out personal information which will then be used illegally.

Precede: Something that comes before.

Reimburse: To repay someone the amount of money they have spent.

Restitution: To repay money taken illegally.

Robocalls: Pre-recorded telephone calls received from a computer auto-dialer.

Scam: To make money by deceiving someone.

Script kiddies: An inexperienced hacker who does not have the skills to launch an attack without the aid of written instructions.

Skimming: The use of a device to capture a user's credit or debit card information.

Smishing: A type of phishing scam that targets Short Message Service (SMS) — text messages — instead of email or phones.

Social Security number: A unique nine-digit number issued by the U.S. government to citizens for identification purposes.

Spam: Unwanted and unsolicited junk email.

Spoof: To deceive by pretending to be someone else.

Spyware: Malicious software installed on a user's computer to gather personal information or track Internet movement.

Surefire: Something that is certain not to fail, or sure to be successful.

Tax returns: A yearly report sent to the government that shows the amount of money earned and the taxes a person paid the previous year.

The Diners Club: Founded in 1950, the Diners Club was the first credit card company. Members used their **Diners Card** to make purchases.

Thief: A person who steals or takes what does not belong to them.

Typosquatting: The deliberate purchasing of an Internet domain name similar to a well-known brand. The purchaser waits for an Internet user to make a typographical error, leading to a site he or she has set up for illegal purposes.

Virus: A type of computer software that causes damage by copying itself and infecting other files or programs.

White hat hacker: An expert computer specialist who uses his skills for good.

White-collar crime: Financially related crimes, usually committed without the threat of physical violence.

Bibliography

"$16 Billion Stolen from 12.7 Million Identity Fraud Victims in 2014." *2015 Identity Fraud Study.* Javelin Strategy & Research, 3 Mar. 2015. Web. 15 Oct. 2016.

"2016 Best Identity Theft Companies." *BestCompany.com.* Bestcompany. com, 2016. Web. 15 Oct. 2016.

"2016 Internet Security Threat Report." *Norton Security Center.* Symantec, 2016. Web. 6 Oct. 2016.

"2016 Underground Hacker Marketplace Report." Dell SecureWorks, Apr. 2016. Web. 27 Sept. 2016.

"Avoiding Technical Support Scams." *Microsoft Safety and Security Center.* Microsoft. Web. 6 Oct. 2016.

"CAPTCHA: Telling Humans and Computers Apart Automatically." *The Official CAPTCHA Site.* Web. 3 Oct. 2016.

"Consumer Information." *Identity Theft Protection Services.* Federal Trade Commission. Web. 15 Oct. 2016.

"Crimeware: Bots." Norton by Symantec, Web. 6 Oct. 2016.

"Easy Definition of Hacking". Cyber.laws.com. Web. 5 Oct. 2016.

"Fake Tiger Sentenced." *DeseretNews.com*. Associated Press, 29 Apr. 2001. Web. 29 Sept. 2016.

"History of Diners Club International." *Dinersclub.com*. Web. 28 Sept. 2016.

"Identity Theft Tops FTC's Consumer Complaint Categories Again in 2014." *Consumer Sentinel Network Data Book*. Federal Trade Commission, 27 Feb. 2015. Web. 27 Sept. 2016.

"IRS's Top Ten Identity Theft Prosecutions; Part of Ongoing Efforts to Protect Taxpayers, Prevent Refund Fraud." Internal Revenue Service, 3 Mar. 2015. Web. 27 Sept. 2016.

"Place Online Fraud Alerts on Your Credit Report." *TransUnion*. TransUnion. Web. 15 Oct. 2016.

"Report Identity Theft." *Federal Trade Commission*. Web. 8 Oct. 2016.

"Smishing and Vishing And Other Cyber Scams to Watch Out for This Holiday " *FBI*. FBI, 24 Nov. 2010. Web. 6 Oct. 2016.

"Stopping Unsolicited Mail, Phone Calls, and Email." *Consumer Information*. Federal Trade Commission. Web. 15 Oct. 2016.

"The Definition of Catfish." Dictionary.com. Web. 15 Oct. 2016.

"The Definition of Escrow." *Merriam-Webster*. Merriam-Webster. Web. 15 Oct. 2016.

"The Definition of Identity Theft." *Merriam-Webster*. Merriam-Webster. Web. 26 Sept. 2016.

"The Definition of Phishing." *Dictionary.com*. Web. 27 Sept. 2016.

"The Invention of the Internet." *History.com*. A&E Television Networks, 2010. Web. 5 Oct. 2016.

"TransUnion." *Credit Report User Guide.* TransUnion, 2015. Web. 15 Oct. 2016.

"Victims of Identity Theft, 2014." Bureau of Justice Statistics, Sept. 2015. Web. 1 Oct. 2016.

"Viruses, Spyware, and Malware." *Information Systems & Technology.* Massachusetts Institute of Technology. Web. 3 Oct. 2016.

"What Is a Computer Virus?" *Microsoft Safety & Security Center.* Microsoft. Web. 3 Oct. 2016.

"What Is Identity Monitoring or "identity Theft Protection" Service?" The Consumer Financial Protection Bureau. Web. 15 Oct. 2016.

"What Is Spyware?" *Microsoft Safety & Security Center.* Microsoft. Web. 5 Oct. 2016.

"White-Collar Crime." Federal Bureau of Investigation, 30 Nov. 2015. Web. 4 Oct. 2016.

Adam Palmer, and Marian Merritt. *2012 Norton Cybercrime Report.* Norton, 2012. Web. 17 Oct. 2016.

Boatman, Kim. "Will Your Teen Fall for These Scams?" *Your Security Resource.* Symantec. Web. 15 Oct. 2016.

Burke, Timothy, and Jack Dickey. "Manti Te'o's Dead Girlfriend, The Most Heartbreaking And Inspirational Story Of The College Football Season, Is A Hoax." *Deadspin.* Gizmodo Media Group, 16 Jan. 2013. Web. 16 Oct. 2016.

Emily Starbuck Gerson and Ben Woolsey. "The History of Credit Cards."- *CreditCards.com.*15 June 2016. Web. 30 Sept. 2016.

Fowler, Janet. "Common Scams Targeted At Teens." *Investopedia.* Investopedia, 09 Oct. 2012. Web. 15 Oct. 2016.

Frank, Mari J. Introduction. *The Complete Idiot's Guide to Recovering from Identity Theft*. New York: Alpha, 2010. 35. Print.

Hunter, Michelle. "Metairie McDonald's Employee Caught Taking Photos of Customer Credit Cards: JPSO." *NOLA.com*. NOLA Media Group, 27 Sept. 2016. Web. 3 Oct. 2016.

Identity Theft and Your Social Security Number. Social Security Administration, 2007. Web. 15 Oct. 2016.

Jiyon. "I, Robot by Isaac Asimov – Review." *The Guardian*. Guardian News and Media, 30 June 2016. Web. 7 Oct. 2016.

Lenhart, Amanda. "About 25 Million People Have Used the Internet to Sell Something." *Pew Research Center Internet Science Tech*. Pew Research Center, 27 Nov. 2005. Web. 15 Oct. 2016.

Lord, Bob. "An Important Message About Yahoo User Security." *Yahoo. tumblr.com*. Yahoo!, 22 Sept. 2016. Web. 3 Oct. 2016.

Maysh, Jeff. " Why One Woman Pretended to Be a High-School Cheerleader." *The Atlantic*. Atlantic Media Company, 6 July 2016. Web. 26 Sept. 2016.

Net Losses: Estimating the Global Cost of Cybercrime: Economic Impact of Cybercrime II. McAfee: Center for Strategic and International Studies, 2014. June 2014. Web. 3 Oct. 2016.

Pajeres, Paul. "Holiday Season Unwraps Phishing, Blackhole Exploit Attacks." *TrendLabs Security Intelligence Blog*. TrendMicro, 02 Jan. 2013. Web. 6 Oct. 2016.

Pascual, Al, Kyle Marchini, and Sarah Miller. "2016 Identity Fraud: Fraud Hits an Inflection Point." *Javelin Strategy & Research*. Javelin, 02 Feb. 2016. Web. 26 Sept. 2016.

Siciliano, Robert. "What Is Typosquatting?" *McAfee Blog Central.* McAfee, 02 July 2013. Web. 6 Oct. 2016.

Swain, Bijay. "What Are Malware, Viruses, Spyware, and Cookies, and What Differentiates Them?" *Symantec Connect.* Symantec, 25 June 2009. Web. 3 Oct. 2016.

Thieves, By Identity. "10 Celebrities Who Got Burned By Identity Thieves." *Business Pundit.* 02 Nov. 2015. Web. 15 Oct. 2016.

Wiederhorn, Jon. "Will Smith Impersonator Lands Three Years Behind Bars." *MTV News.* MTV, 16 Dec. 2002. Web. 27 Sept. 2016.

Index

Myra Faye Turner is a freelance writer and the author of the poetry collection, *Poems in Progress*. As the mother of a teen son, she is very concerned about identity theft. She is careful to guard his personal information so that it does not fall into the wrong hands. She and her son, Tyler, live in New Orleans.